HAL LEONARD
BASS METHOD

F

CW00546119

by CHRIS KRINGEL

To access audio visit:
www.halleonard.com/mylibrary

"Enter Code"
"2267-4914-6297-0863"

ISBN 978-1-4950-5880-6

HAL•LEONARD®
CORPORATION

7777 W. BLUEMOUND RD. P.O. BOX 13819 MILWAUKEE, WI 53213

Visit Hal Leonard Online at **www.halleonard.com**

INTRODUCTION

Welcome to the Hal Leonard *Funk Bass Method*. This book is designed to teach you some of the many skills needed to become a great funk bassist. I will focus mainly on the slap and pop style of funk bass playing. Later, we'll move into the area of fingerstyle funk, as well as grooving and soloing in the funk idiom. As you begin to work through this book, you'll notice that what sets this funk bass method apart from other funk bass books is the use of real songs—by some of the greatest funk slap and pop bassists of the past and present—in helping to demonstrate each technique and concept for you. So let's get started!

How Funk Started

Funk music is a mixture of soul, rhythm and blues, and jazz. Funk as a music style came into its own in the '60s, and continued to develop into the '70s and beyond. The typical funk song of the late '60s and '70s was big on the bass and drums, peppered with some scratchy guitar riffs, keys, and usually vocals. The key element of funk is groove, pure and simple, particularly the bass and drum groove. Major rhythmic components of the funk style include syncopation and the triplet (or swing) feel.

Upright bass players—from as far back as the 1920s—who slapped strings against the necks of their basses in a percussive manner (simulating a drummer), essentially started the slap and pop style of funk bass. In the late '60s, slap and pop was introduced to the electric bass by Larry Graham, bassist for Sly and the Family Stone and later Graham Central Station. Several other great bass players who have adopted Larry's style and even taken it to new heights are Louis Johnson, Stanley Clarke, Marcus Miller, Mark King, and more currently, Flea and Victor Wooten to mention a few.

Larry Graham

Marcus Miller

Louis Johnson

Practicing

Practicing music is like practicing a sport. You have to put time in to get results! The reason you play a sport is for enjoyment. To excel in the game, you must practice the different aspects of the game. Likewise, to excel at funk bass, you will need to practice the different aspects of bass playing.

Let's stay with the sports analogy just a bit longer. Learning the rules of the game for a basketball player is like learning music theory for a bass player. Learning the proper way to dribble and shoot a basketball is comparable to developing proper bass technique. Understanding different plays and court strategies is like understanding different musical styles and idioms. If you've forgotten the plays because you didn't mentally prepare, you might just crash and burn. The more you can put your understanding and practice time onto the court, the better your game becomes. With more practice, your basketball playing and your bass playing will become instinctual. You will be able to surrender to the moment. You create, you move, you act and react. The more you know, the less you'll need to think about the game rules. You can then surrender to the moment and create, move, act, and react instinctually. If you are weak in certain areas of the game, like technique, sooner or later you'll have to shoot a free throw.

The Four Types of Practice

1. Technical: Proficiency of finger movement over the strings of the instrument in playing particular notes with clarity and control. The more proficient you are at finger techniques, the more freely you will be able to express your musical ideas.

2. Mental: Learning how to put it all together, the notes, the scales, the theory and concepts. Absorbing other aspects of music besides instrument practice will strengthen your overall musicality greatly and give you the wherewithal to act and react when new situations arise.

3. Auditory: Listening to music and developing a "good ear" is essential in becoming a great bass player. This might be learning to hear and recognize intervals and chord changes or transcribing music by ear to paper. Trained listening enables you to express yourself more fully and is extremely important in the evolution of your overall musical abilities.

4. Playing: Putting it all together, the technical, mental, and auditory. From practicing sight-reading, to improvising, or to jamming just for fun, you will need to link everything together to create great music.

Metronomes and Drum Machines

Practicing with a time reference point like a metronome or drum machine helps to develop a good "time feel." You are human, so without an external tempo reference of some sort you will most likely tend to speed up or slow down, sometimes a lot and sometimes a little. The place you will want to get to is to stay as close to exact time as possible.

As a bassist, your job is to keep time with the drummer (or by yourself if you don't have a drummer). By practicing with an external time reference point on a regular basis, you will learn to hear this external clock in an internal way. Timing is everything.

Audio

Through each chapter you will have audio accompaniment with a metronome, drum machine, or drummer, and at the end of each chapter you will have a full band to jam along with. The bass will be panned hard right so that you can pan your stereo hard left and play along with the tracks, minus the recorded bass. If the exercises are too slow or too fast, practice them with a metronome or drum machine for best results. The corresponding track number for each example or song is listed below the audio icon.

Tuning Up

Let's tune up by playing the open strings E, A, D, and G.

TRACK 1

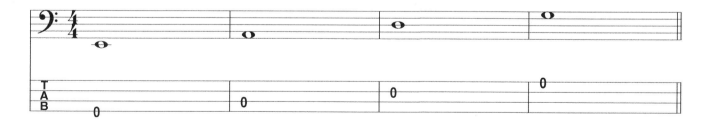

Bass Position

When playing bass, the position that the instrument sits on your body is extremely important. The height on your body and the left-to-right balance of your bass should be the same standing or sitting, especially when playing slap and pop style. If it isn't, what you practice sitting down will be hard to do while standing up, or vice-versa.

Placement

There are two ways to rest the instrument on your body if you are seated. Centered on your body, and off center toward your plucking hand. To play in the seated, centered position (if you are right handed) you'd place the bass on your left thigh after slightly elevating your left leg. To play in the off center position, place the bass slightly to the right side of your body with the bass resting on your right thigh.

Sitting / Center

Standing / Center

Sitting / Right

Standing / Right

Angle

The angle at which you hold your bass will effect the way you play. It's best to find the angle that is most comfortable for you. Some players actually change the angle of their bass depending on which technique they are executing. When playing the slap and pop technique, most players hold their bass almost horizontal or level with the floor so their plucking or slapping hand is more comfortable. Some players hold their bass at a 45-degree angle because it is more comfortable on their fretting hand. The idea is to create the most efficient and comfortable position without strain.

Almost Level

45 Degrees

THUMB SLAP

The thumb slap is simply that… slapping your thumb against the strings. This is actually the trickiest part of slap and pop, so take your time to get it down right. Take your hand and make a fist. Now stick your thumb out. It should look like you're about to hitchhike a ride or like you are giving someone the "thumbs up" sign. You will be striking the string with the first joint of your thumb, the one just behind your fingernail.

Slap Position

Point of Contact

Now let's work on attacking the string with the thumb. You will be striking the string against the edge of the fingerboard. There are two ways to execute this movement and either is fine. We'll label them as "the bounce" and "the follow through." The first one, the **bounce**, involves striking the string directly in an up-down motion. The key to this movement is to strike the string and bounce off quickly so that the string rings. The second technique, the **follow through**, involves striking the string in a downward motion and following through until your thumb comes to rest on the string below the one you have just struck. In both cases strike the string hard enough so it gives off a percussive sound, not a plucking sound.

The most important part of the thumb slap is that you *do not move your thumb.* The movement actually comes from your wrist/forearm, not your hand. To give you an idea of how this works, place your thumbs-up sign on a table, with your thumb in the air. Now hit the table with your thumb by twisting your forearm, not by bending your wrist. This is the movement you will want to achieve.

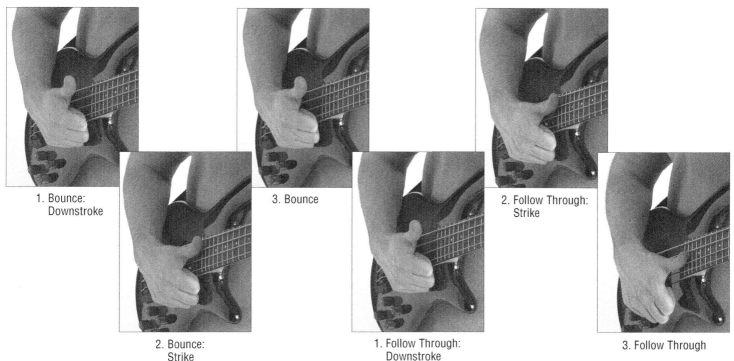

1. Bounce: Downstroke

2. Bounce: Strike

3. Bounce

1. Follow Through: Downstroke

2. Follow Through: Strike

3. Follow Through

Let's give it a try. In this example you'll hear how it should and shouldn't sound as you slap your thumb against the E string. The first measure of this example shows how you will want a thumb slap to sound. The second measure is played wrong so that you can hear what it sounds like if you don't bounce or follow through quickly enough.

A thumb slap is indicated with a "T" in between the tab and notation staves.

TRACK 2

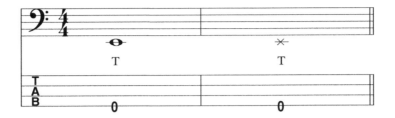

Thumb Slap Accuracy

Now let's work on getting a nice, clean tone while slapping all the strings.

TRACK 3

When you feel as though you can get through these exercises with a clean, fluid motion, it's time to move on. These are great exercises to go back to and gradually increase the metronome or drum machine speeds. Being able to play at slow and fast tempos with the same accuracy and clarity is essential in becoming a good funk player.

Thumb Slap Exercises

As stated before, the most important technique in slap and pop is the thumb slap. I'm not kidding! It's essential that you are able to produce a clean and fluid tone before moving into string popping. For the next few exercises let's change rhythms, skip strings, and start increasing some tempos.

TRACK 5
(cont'd)

TRACK 6

8

Now that you have command of the thumb slap, let's move into some real songs! A great way to practice the thumb slap is to play songs that you can currently play fingerstyle, but play them with the thumb slap instead. I don't recommend that you do this at gigs or rehearsals with a band; the best place to practice new techniques with songs that you already know is at home. "Let's Groove" is a funk classic by Earth, Wind & Fire that was originally played fingerstyle. We'll perform it with the thumb slap so that you can get an idea of how this may work.

TRACK 7

LET'S GROOVE

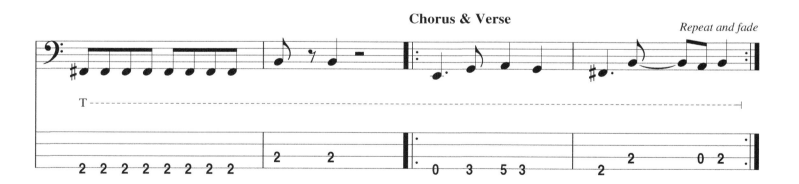

This next song was performed by The Ohio Players, and again it was originally played fingerstyle. Give this song a shot!

FIRE

TRACK 8

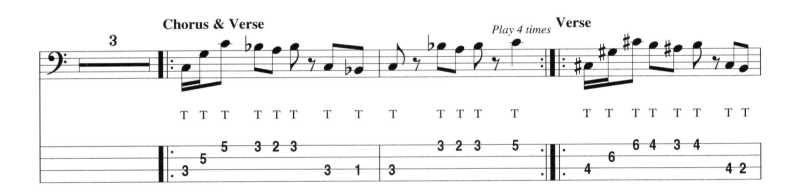

Words and Music by Ralph Middlebrooks, Marshall Jones, Leroy Bonner, Clarence Satchell, Willie Beck and Marvin Pierce
Copyright © 1974 by Play One Music Publishing
Copyright Renewed
All Rights Administered by Unichappell Music Inc.
International Copyright Secured   All Rights Reserved

FINGER POP

The finger pop is, essentially, snapping the strings with one of your fingers to create a *pop* sound. You can use either your index or middle finger to execute the finger pop. Experiment to find out which finger feels more comfortable. You might actually want to use them both, but we'll explore that later on in this book.

So let's get back to the hitchhiker thumb or the thumbs-up sign. Loosen up your index or middle finger and create a hook with whichever finger you choose.

Index Finger Pop

Middle Finger Pop

Hand placement for popping is directly above the fingerboard. This works great in tandem with the thumb slap as well because once your extended thumb slaps the string, you can follow up with a finger pop in one fluid movement. Don't do it quite yet though… get your popping clean first, and then move forward to combine the two techniques. When finger popping, you will want to get a nice, clean pop or snap sound from the string. Place just enough of your finger under the string to grab it, and pull up. Make sure you pull just enough to get that sound. Popping too hard might break the string, and popping too softly will sound like a pluck, not a pop. So listen for that in-between sound, not too hard, not too soft, but just right.

1. Finger Pop: Setup

2. Finger Pop: Grab

3. Finger Pop: Snap

Let's give it a try! A pop is indicated by a "P" in between the tab and notation staves.

TRACK 9

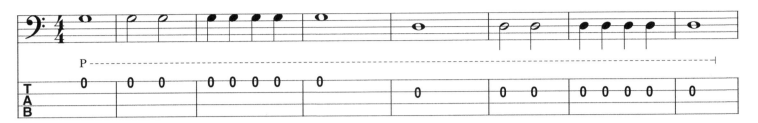

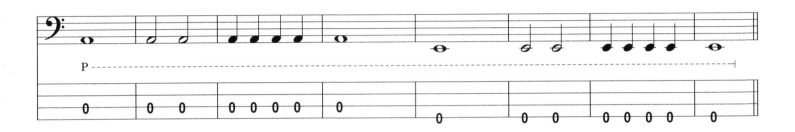

Muting

Now let's work on solving a problem that might arise when popping the strings. String ring is the problem, and muting is the remedy! To mute the strings after you pop, use your fretting hand to touch the string just enough to stop the string from vibrating. Sounds easy enough, doesn't it? So let's try muting in the next exercise. Wherever you see a rest, touch the string with a finger on your fretting hand to stop the sound.

TRACK 10

Finger Pop Exercises

Let's do some exercises for finger popping. Again we'll mix it up with some string skipping, and be sure to mute the strings during the rests.

TRACK 11

TRACK 11
(cont'd)

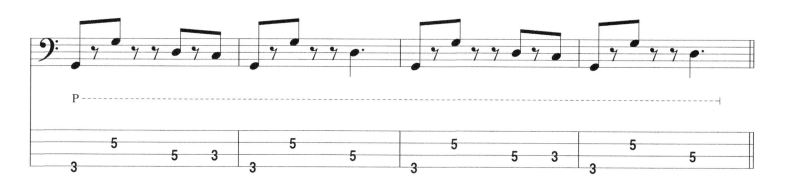

Let's try finger popping in a song. This song by The Staple Singers is played fingerstyle with some finger pops added on the accents.

I'LL TAKE YOU THERE

Words and Music by Alvertis Isbell
Copyright © 1972 IRVING MUSIC, INC.
Copyright Renewed
All Rights Reserved   Used by Permission

SLAP AND POP

When combining slap and pop, remember to make it happen in one fluid movement! As you start downward to slap with your thumb, pull up with a pop from your finger. It's trickier than it sounds and takes some time to get right. Remember, it's important to make the movement from your forearm, and not from your wrist or hand.

1. Slap: Downstroke

2. Slap: Strike

3. Pop: Grab

4. Pop: Snap

Try this and listen for the sound quality. I'll slap an open E string and pop the E (an octave up) on the 2nd fret of the D string. When you do this make sure both notes ring.

TRACK 13

Octaves

When slapping, octaves are king. The best way to practice slapping and popping in the same movement is to play octaves. The word octave means, "eight notes apart." These are used in funk all the time, as in the previous example where I played the same E note an octave apart, slapping the lower note and popping the E an octave higher.

Let's try a few octave exercises. Make sure you play the thumb slaps and finger pops with clean attacks so the notes ring out clearly.

TRACK 14

Slap and Pop Exercises

Next let's use octaves along with some other exercises, like slapping and popping on the same string, and then on the adjacent strings.

TRACK 15

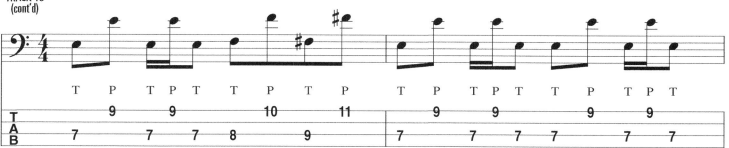

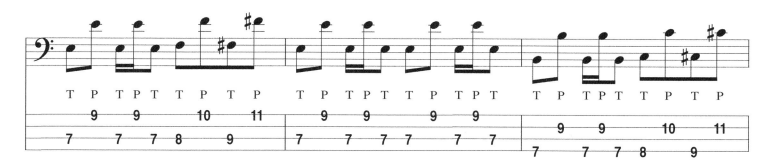

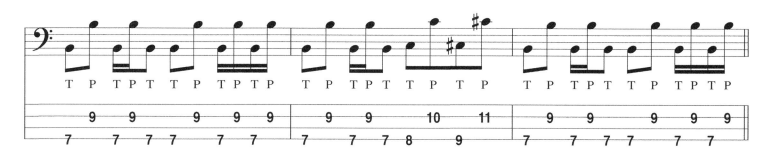

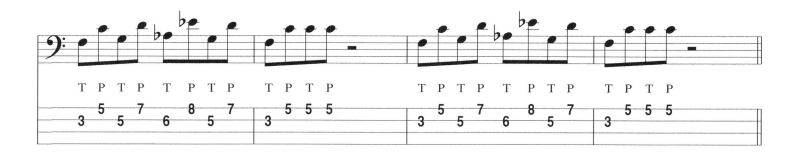

Let's play some tunes that combine slap and pop!

This song was originally written and recorded by Stevie Wonder and later covered by The Red Hot Chili Peppers. This is a great example of slap and pop.

HIGHER GROUND

TRACK 17

This song by Jeffrey Osborne is another great example of slap and pop.

STAY WITH ME TONIGHT

TRACK 18

Let's play a song that was originally done fingerstyle and add the slap and pop style to it. This song is "Brick House" by the Commodores.

BRICK HOUSE

TRACK 19

TECHNIQUES

In this chapter I'll break down some techniques that are used in the slap and pop idiom. These can also be applied to finger-style as well as other styles, so you're getting twice the bang for your buck. Master these techniques and they become a way of expressing yourself.

Hammer-On

To play a hammer-on, place one of your fingers on a fret and thumb slap or finger pop that note. While the note is still ringing, hammer down on that string higher up with another fret-hand finger, sounding a second note higher in pitch. The force of the hammer-on causes that new note to ring without slapping or popping again.

Let's try this with an example. With my first finger, I'll fret the note C on the 3rd fret of the A string and thumb slap, then I'll hammer down with my third finger on a D note (5th fret). After the thumb slap, I'll do it again but this time with a finger pop at the same location. The trick is to give both notes the same dynamic or loudness.

1. Hammer-On: Setup   2. Hammer-On: Execution

TRACK 20

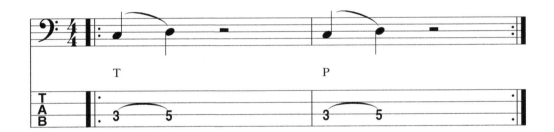

Hammer-On Exercises

Let's do some exercises using the hammer-on technique.

TRACK 21

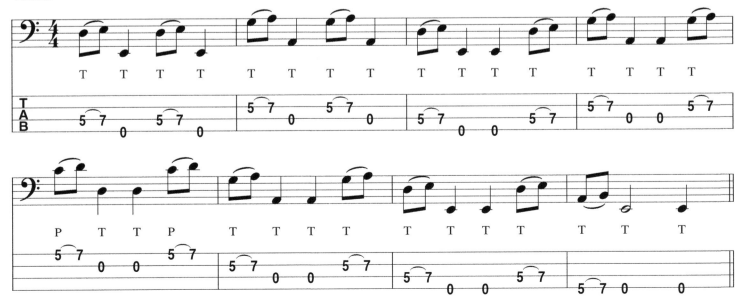

24

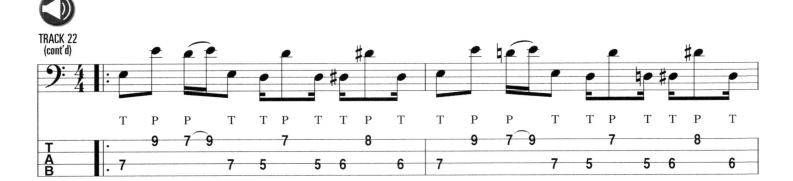

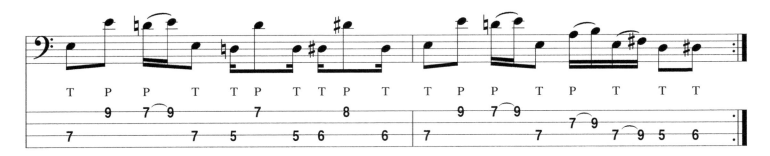

Pull-Off

To play a pull-off, place two of your fret-hand fingers on different frets of the same string and thumb slap or finger pop the note higher in pitch. While that note is ringing, pull your higher fret finger off the string sideways without releasing the pressure on the string. The other finger holds down the lower-pitched note, and the force of the pull-off causes that lower note to ring without another thumb slap or finger pop attack.

Here's an example of how this should sound. I'll thumb slap the note D on the 5th fret of the A string, fretting it with my third finger, then pulling off to the note C (3rd fret) that my first finger is already holding down. After the thumb slap I'll do it again, but this time with a finger pop at the same location. Remember, the trick is to play both notes with the same dynamic or loudness.

1. Pull Off: Setup   2. Pull Off: Execution

TRACK 23

Pull-Off Exercises

Let's move into some examples to get things rolling.

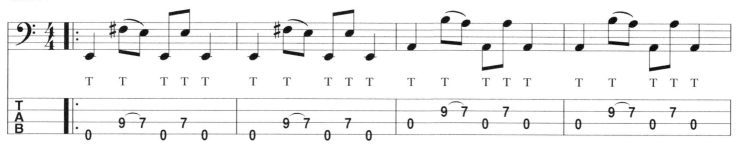

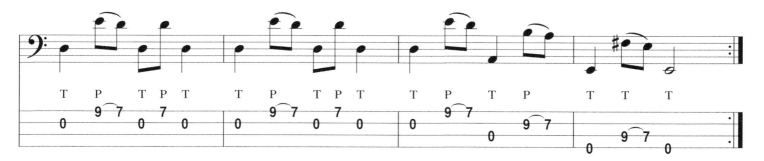

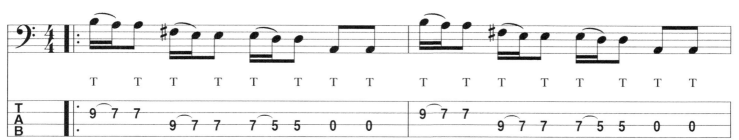

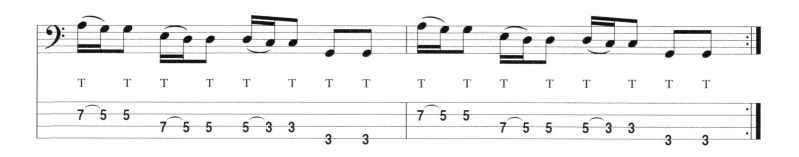

Combining Hammer-Ons and Pull-Offs

Now I'll combine both the hammer-on and pull-off in some examples.

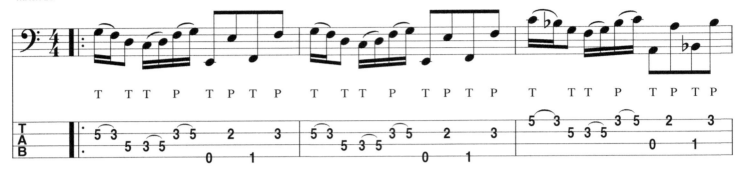

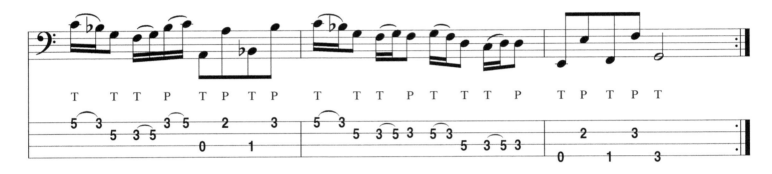

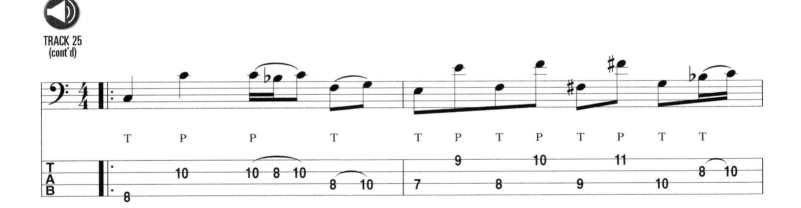

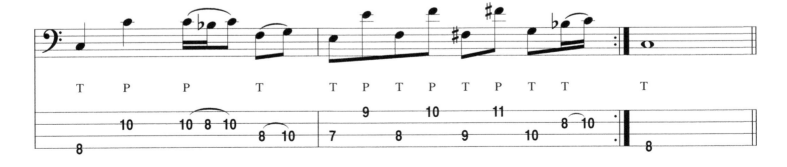

Dead Notes

A dead note is just that, a dead sound, meaning it has no pitch. Dead notes are used as a percussive noise to add rhythm and vibe to a bass line while slapping. The way to achieve a dead note is to mute the note with your fretting hand by touching the string (but without actually fretting any notes) while slapping or popping.

Dead Note Slap

Let's play a dead note slap. I'll place my fretting hand over the note G, on the 3rd fret of the E string. The key is to not press down with the fretting hand, but to just touch the string in the middle of the fret. If your finger is too close to a fret, or if you depress the string too hard, you'll inadvertently produce a harmonic. If you don't touch it hard enough the string will still ring, so be careful.

TRACK 27

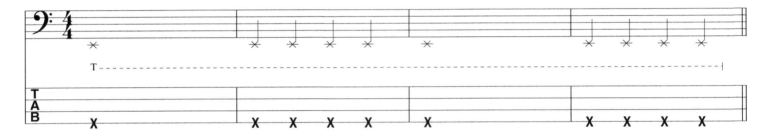

Let's do some exercises with the dead note slap.

TRACK 28

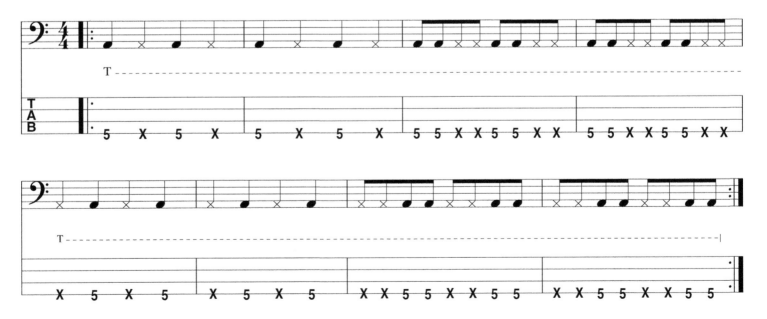

Dead Note Pop

Let's play a dead note pop. I'll place my fretting hand over the note A on the 2nd fret of the G string. Be really careful to not press down with the fretting finger on the dead note pop because the pop has a tendency to produce overtones and harmonics more so than the slap.

TRACK 30

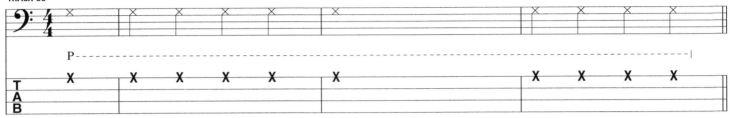

Here are some exercises using dead note pops.

TRACK 31

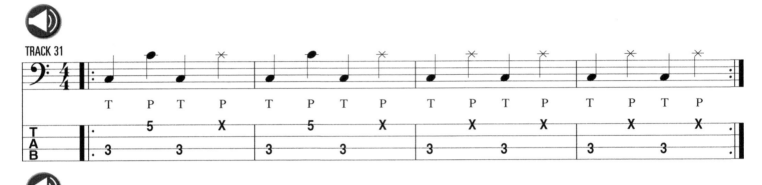

TRACK 31
(cont'd)

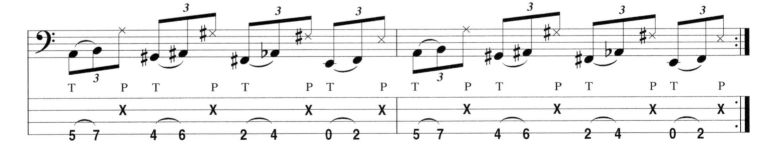

Now let's combine dead note slaps and pops.

TRACK 32

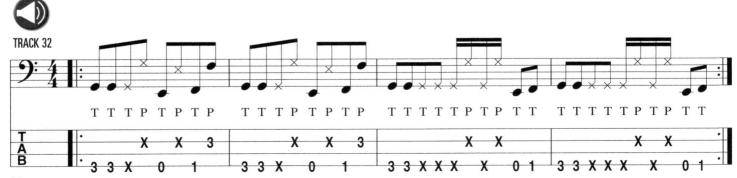

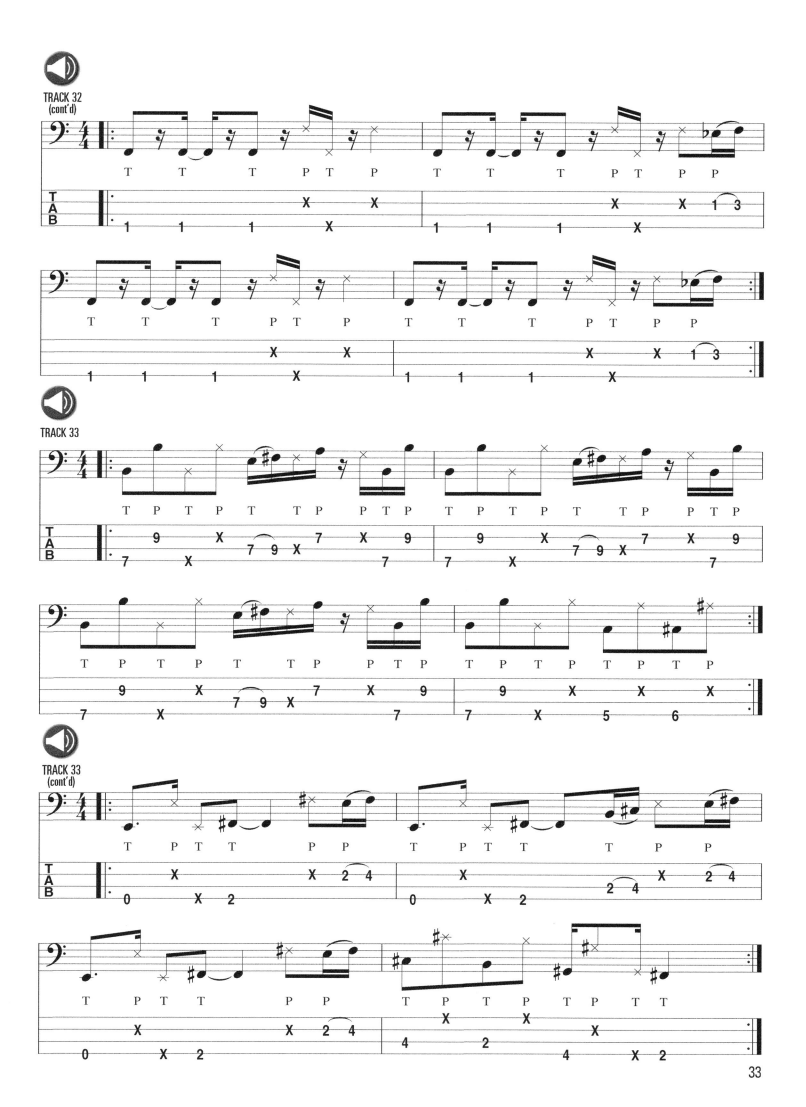

Now that you have covered dead notes, hammer-ons, and pull-offs, it will open up a whole new range of songs that you can play in the funk bass slap and pop style. Let's move into some songs where you can make good use of these techniques. This song is by Level 42, whose lead singer/bass player influenced a great deal of players in the slap/pop idiom.

HOT WATER

TRACK 34

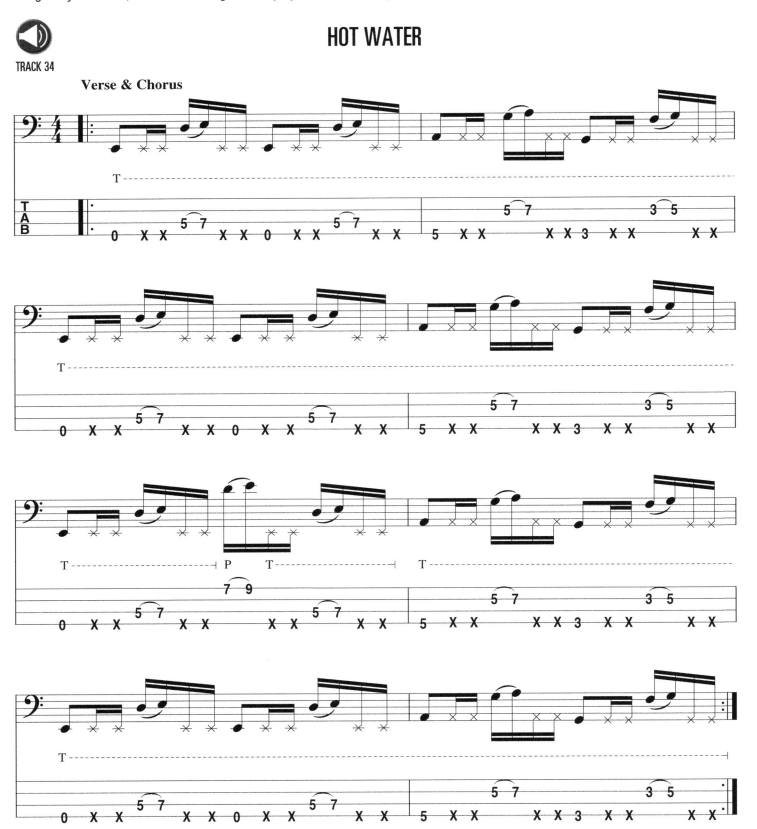

Bridge

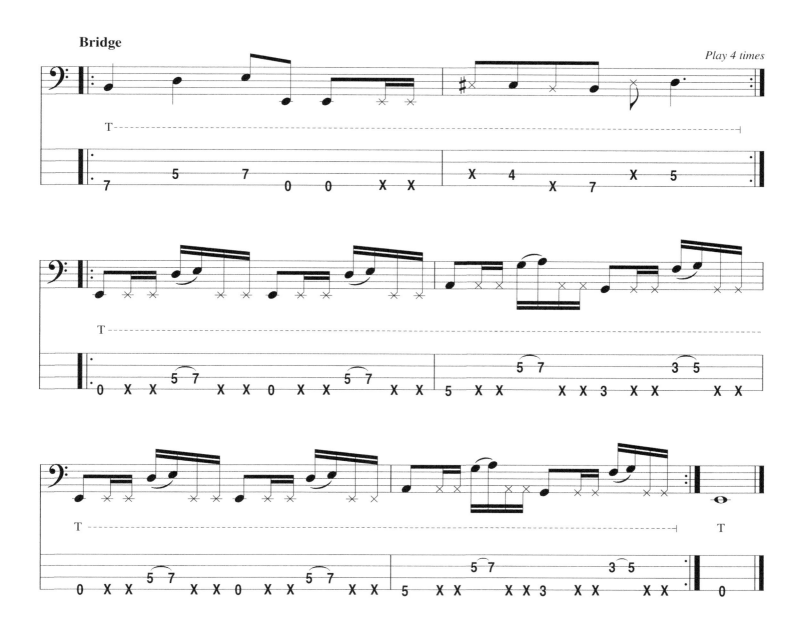

Another Chili Peppers song!

TRACK 35

CAN'T STOP

Words and Music by Anthony Kiedis, Flea, John Frusciante and Chad Smith
© 2002 MOEBETOBLAME MUSIC

Slides

Another great way to add spice to a funk bass line is to slide from one note to another, either ascending or descending in pitch. To perform a slide, play a note slap or pop, then without lifting your finger off the string, slide your finger either up or down the fretboard, ascending or descending to the target note. There are two types of slides, a grace note slide, which is so quick that it has no real rhythmic value, and a regular slide, which does have a rhythmic value.

We'll try an example with slides both ascending and descending so that you can hear the difference. First I'll play a grace note slide, then a regular slide. Listen carefully to where the note starts on the grace slide versus the regular.

TRACK 36

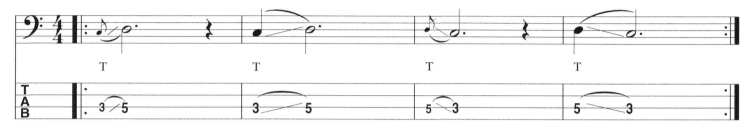

Here are some exercises to help you get this under your belt.

TRACK 37

TRACK 37
(cont'd)

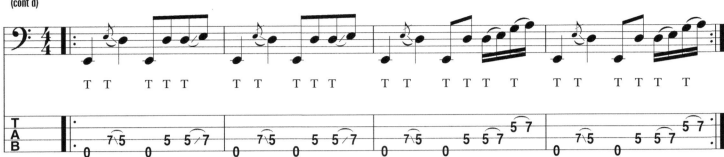

I'll play both an ascending and descending slide for this one.

TRACK 38

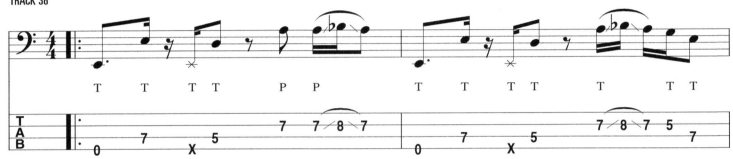

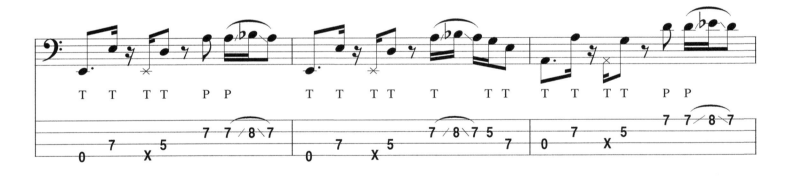

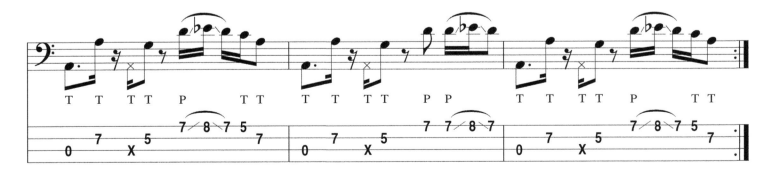

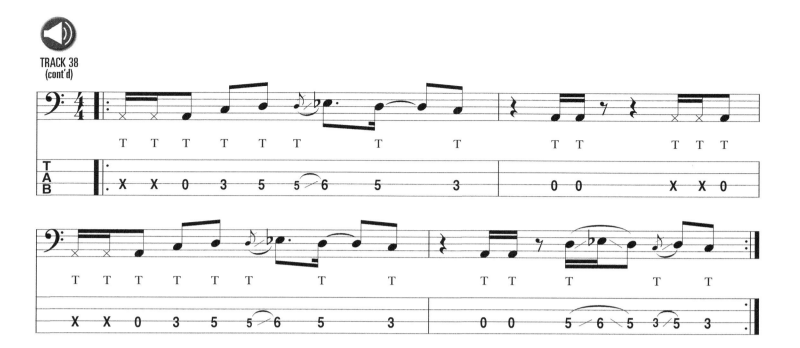

Trills

A trill is another way to add a little bit of vibe to a funk line. To execute a trill, place one of the fingers from your fretting hand on a note. While fretting the note, hammer on and pull off at a rapid pace with one of your other fingers on a higher fret.

On this example, I'll place the first finger of my fret hand on a C at the 5th fret of the G string, then I'll hammer on and pull off of the D on the 7th fret of the same string. Now you give it a shot!

1. Trill: Setup

3. Trill: Pull String

2. Trill: Hammer On

4. Trill: Pull Off

TRACK 39

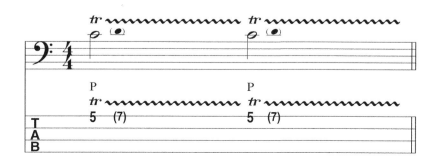

When you feel comfortable with the trill try this next exercise.

TRACK 39
(cont'd)

Vibrato

Another great technique for adding a little soul to your line is vibrato. Vibrato is widely used by guitar players and nearly as often by bassists. It can range from very subtle to very noticeable depending on what you are trying to project. It can add a singing quality to your bass line. Vibrato is achieved by first playing a note, then pushing and pulling that string with the fret-hand back and forth as the note rings. Here is how it sounds. The first example has a very subtle vibrato, and in the second it is more noticeable.

TRACK 40

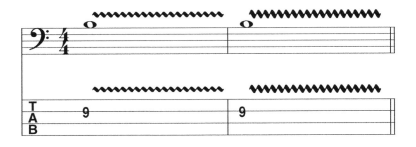

Now let's try it in an exercise.

TRACK 40
(cont'd)

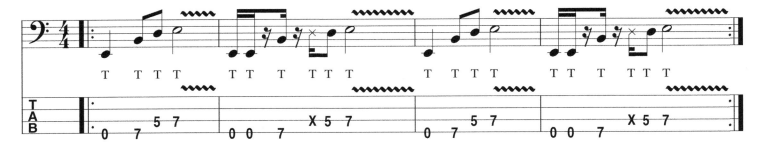

Shakes

A shake sounds much like a trill but with a slide added, creating a hipper, funkier sound. Essentially, you pop a note, and instead of trilling with two fingers, you slide back and forth with one finger at a rapid pace.

For the next example, I'll pop a D on the 7th fret of the G string, and with the first finger of my fretting hand, I'll slide back and forth from the D note to an E♭ on the 8th fret of the same string.

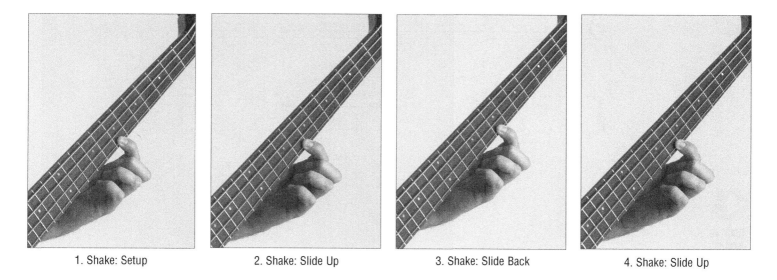

1. Shake: Setup   2. Shake: Slide Up   3. Shake: Slide Back   4. Shake: Slide Up

TRACK 41

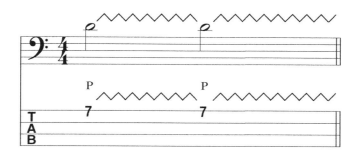

This is the shake in a bass line.

TRACK 41
(cont'd)

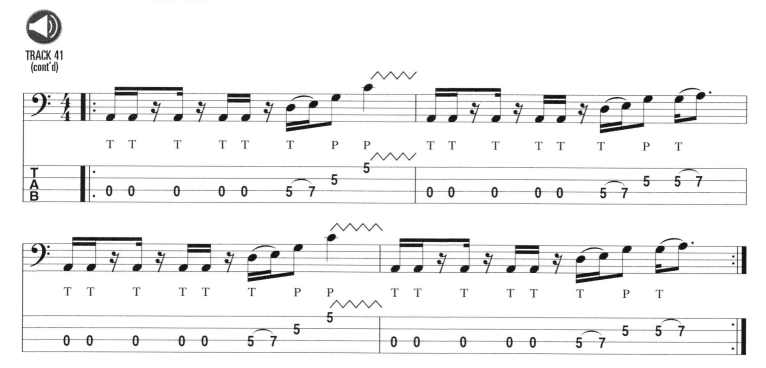

41

Bends

Like vibrato, bends are widely used by guitar players. Bends can range from full step bends (or more) to one-quarter step bends depending on what you are trying to project. Bends are achieved by pushing or pulling the sounding string(s) in one direction with the fret hand, creating a whole new pitch that is sustained for however long the bend is held. Here is how it sounds.

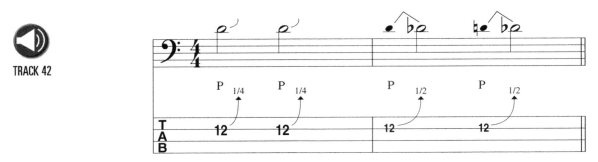

TRACK 42

A bend in a groove!

TRACK 42
(cont'd)

Technique Exercises

Now let's get into some functional bass lines that include slides, vibrato, trills, shakes, and bends.

TRACK 43

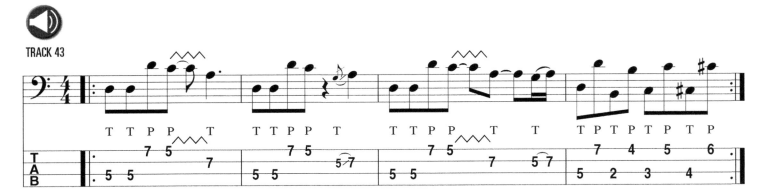

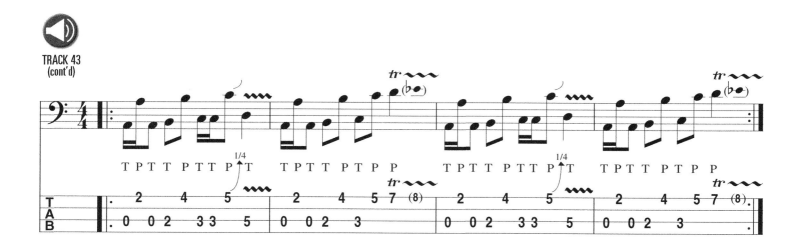

TRACK 44

Left-Hand Slap

The fret-hand slap is often referred to as the left-hand slap. To achieve this technique, slap your fretting hand against the fingerboard to create a percussive sound similar to a dead note slap. Just like the regular slap, you'll want a bounce-like motion so that you don't actually fret a note. Flatten your fingers as much as possible and slap them all simultaneously against the fingerboard. Use a left-hand slap in conjunction with a regular thumb slap and you will come up with some pretty killer grooves.

1. LH Slap: Setup

2. LH Slap: Strike

3. LH Slap: Bounce Back

Listen to the next track. I'll play a fret-hand slap first the right way, and then the wrong way. Listen carefully to the difference so that when you're practicing, you will know what sound to develop. It can be a bit tricky and may take some time to get right. This technique is indicated by an "L" in between the tab and notation staves.

TRACK 45

Now I'll move into some exercises that will gradually get harder. The first one is in a triplet pattern, and is a standard fill for funk lines. Start slow and build up the tempo. This is a great movement to get under your fingers. In this example, I'll play it at three different tempos so that you can hear how it sounds slow, medium, and fast before moving on to other examples.

TRACK 46

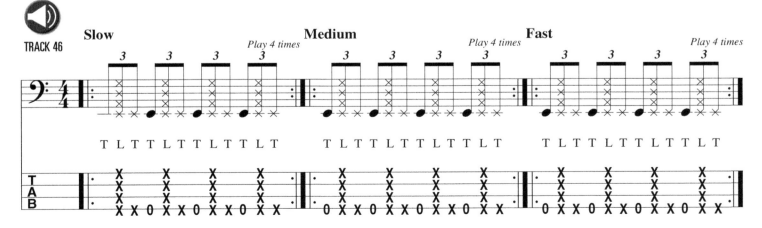

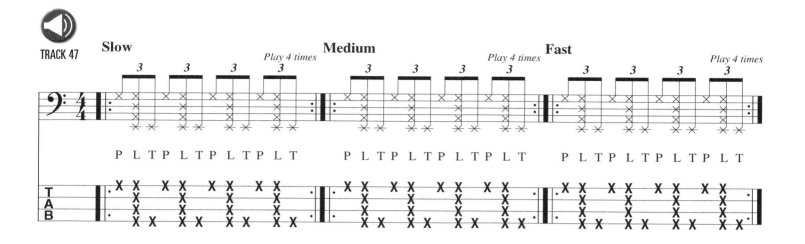

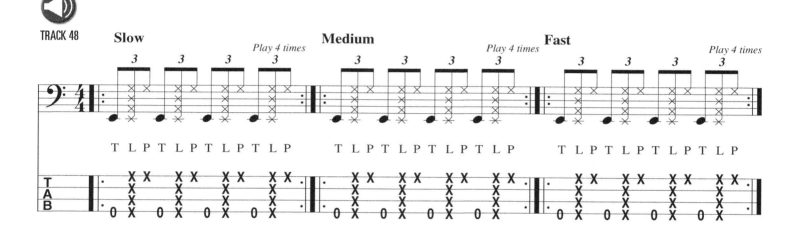

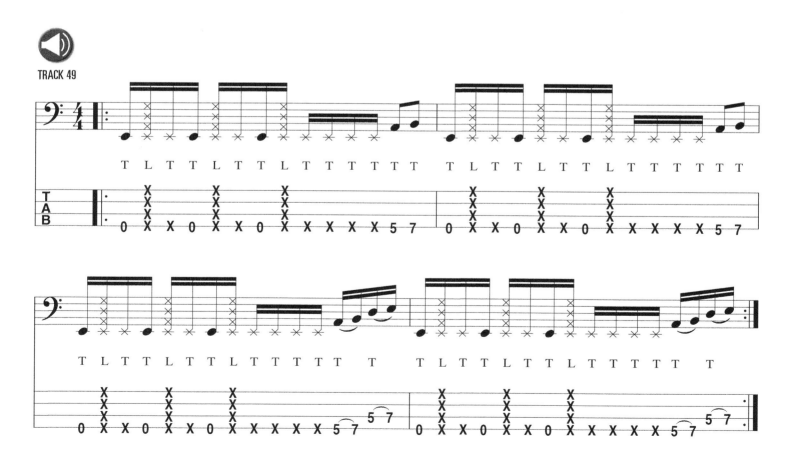

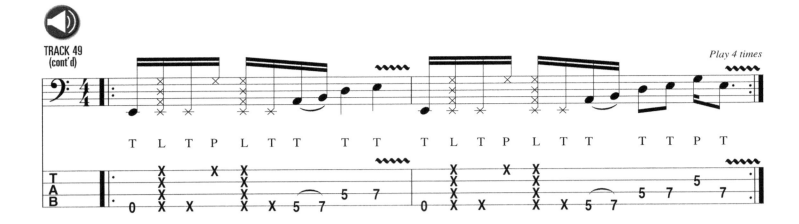

Open Strings

In slap bass, open strings can really help you to move around and make those funk lines and fills sound super big! In the next examples I'll combine hammer-ons and open strings to give you an idea of how to use open strings to fill up your sound. Let the open strings ring out.

TRACK 50

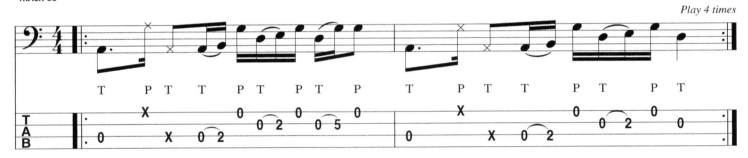

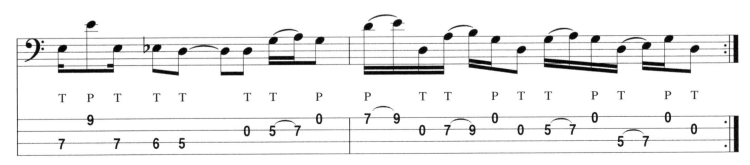

To review these techniques, let's play some songs. Remember that these are great techniques for adding vibe, funk, and a little excitement to a song and bass line, but, too much of a good thing can ruin the song and take away from the groove that you've worked so hard to establish. Listen first, and if it feels like a good idea, then add a little something. A big key to funk slap bass is building up a vocabulary of slap and pop licks, as well as other various techniques, that you can instinctively "say" to enhance the music. Start by learning the ones in this book and listening to other players. Gradually you will build and change them around to come up with your own.

Another Level 42 song with the left-hand slap in the opening groove.

LOVE GAMES

TRACK 52

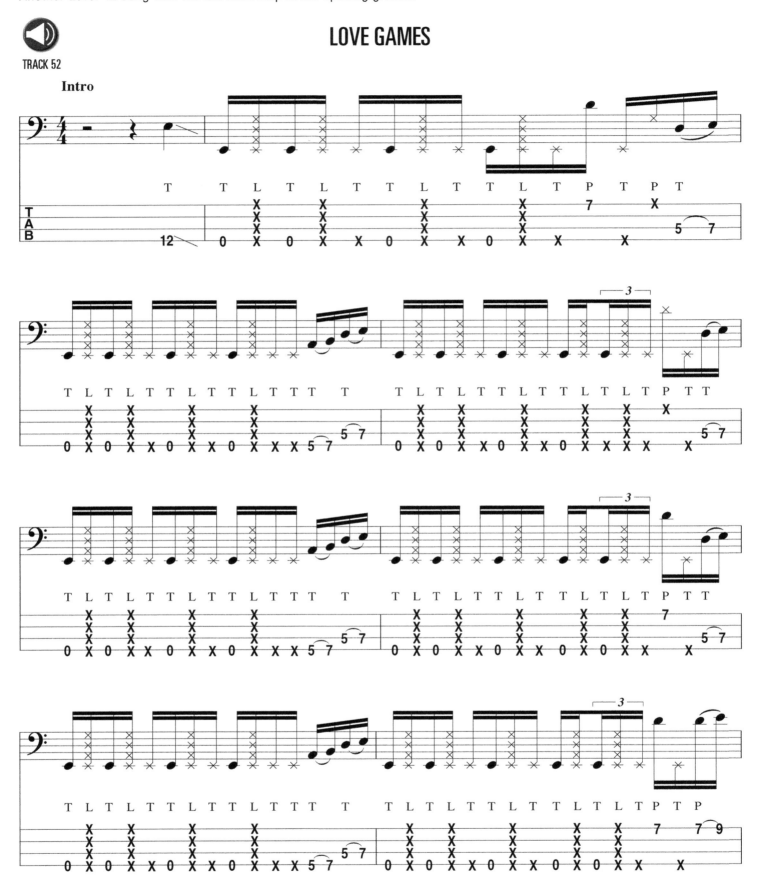

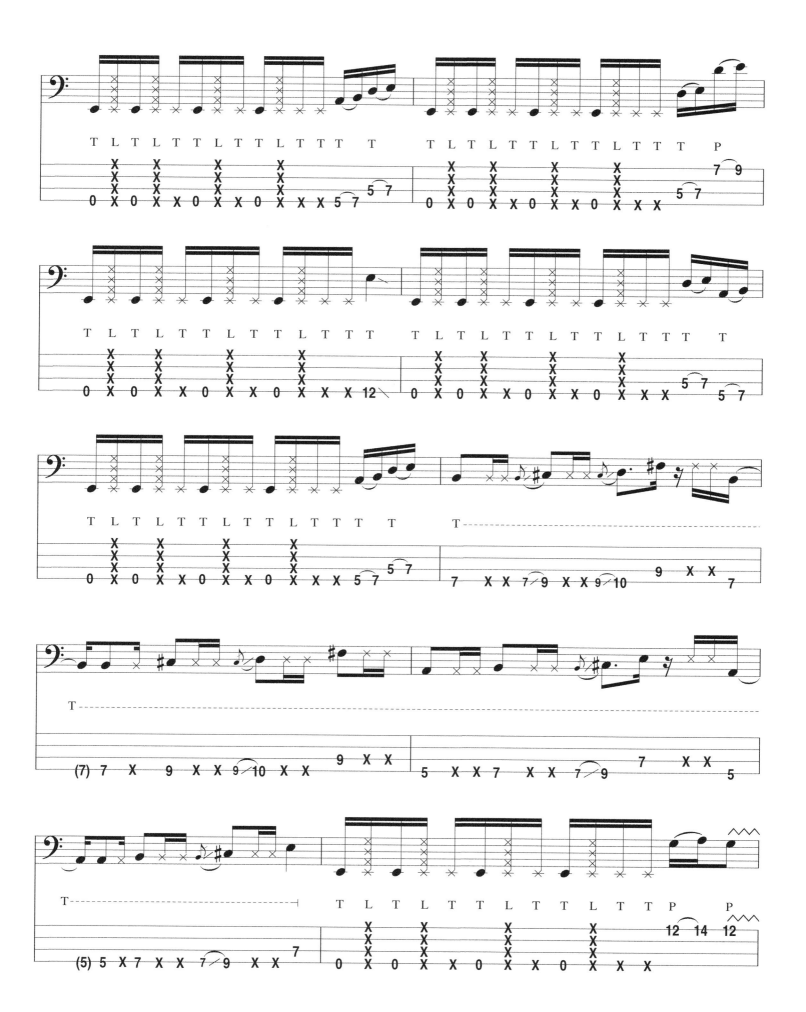

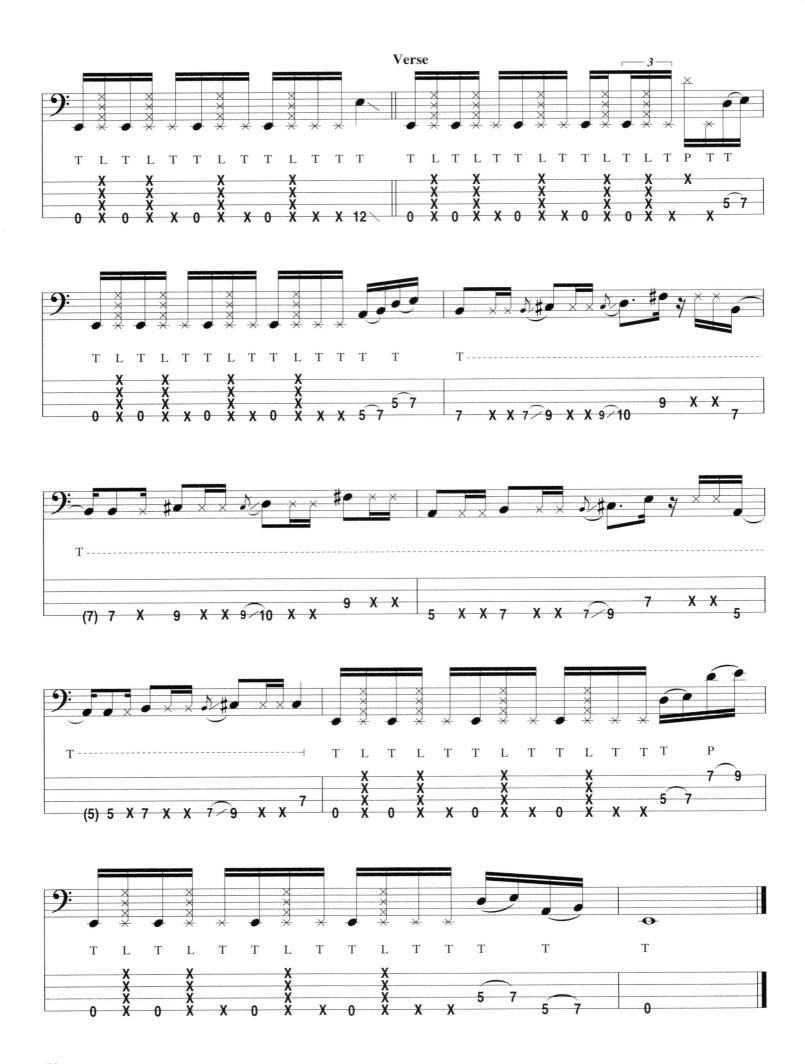

This song is a perfect example of how certain rock bands take slap lines and incorporate them into a song. This one is by the band 311.

COME ORIGINAL

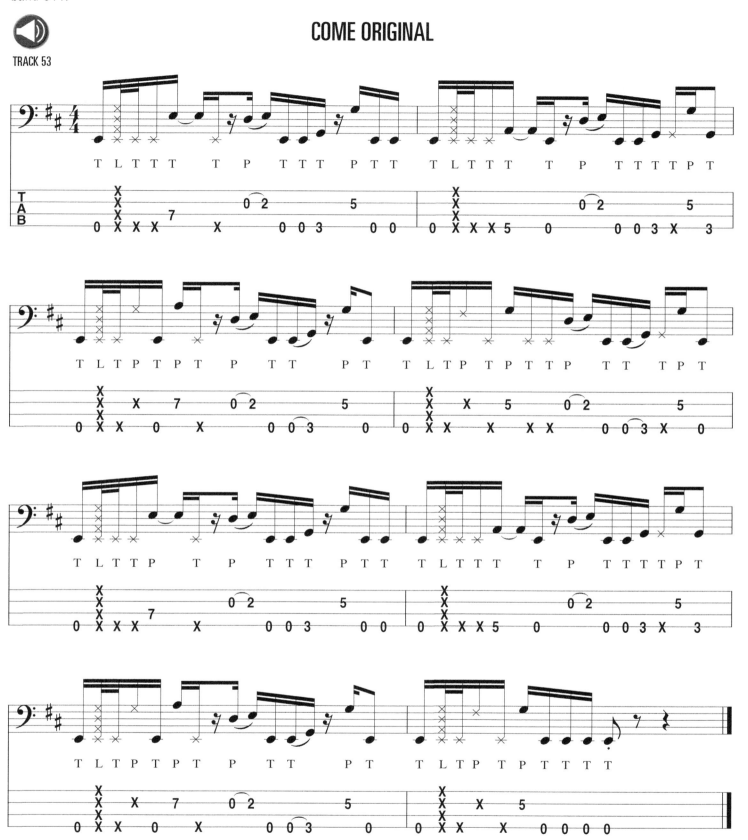

Music by Nicholas Hexum and Aaron Wills
Lyrics by Nicholas Hexum and Doug Martinez
Copyright © 1999 by Hydroponic Music
All Rights Reserved   Used by Permission

GROOVING

In this chapter we'll look at the concept or ability to groove. To a musician, groove means to lay down a path that the rest of the band can sink into. Imagine yourself cutting a groove in a piece of wood that everything around it falls into. The way a bassist approaches the groove has a dramatic effect on the whole band. As a bassist, this may be the word you've heard or will hear more than any other word in your entire life! Many artists say that you can't teach someone how to groove. Often bassists don't groove because they have not looked into why a line isn't grooving. If you look at timing, feel, and attack, this might help you to interpret the groove. Let's also bring fingerstyle into the picture so that you can concentrate on grooving. This book is about funk, and funk is about having the groove and feel.

Staccato or Legato

The duration of a note can have a huge effect on the groove. Whether you play a note long and for its full duration, or short and abrupt, this can change the entire scope of a groove. Staccato means to play a note short in length, and legato is to play a note for its full duration. Imagine a backdrop on a stage. The color and design of the backdrop sets an unconscious mood or vibe for whatever happens on that stage. It catches your eye differently and sets a mood depending on the color used, or if it has a pattern instead of a solid color. The same concept can apply to note duration and whether they are played staccato or legato; these sound "colors" can set an audible mood and vibe.

Staccato

A staccato note is indicated in notation by placing a dot under or above the note. The rhythm would otherwise be written with a large number of rests in between the notes to account for these specific gaps in sound. Adding the staccato dot is often easier than notating every rest. Playing staccato leaves space in between the notes for everything else to stick out. You can think of it as almost adding more rhythm to the drum part. Staccato would be like our stage backdrop with a pattern on it, not a solid color. Staccato notes can also add some serious attitude to the feel of a song by creating a tight and abrupt funky groove.

Legato

Playing legato is usually implied. If it is marked at all, it is done with a short line under or above the note. Playing long, full notes lays down a solid foundation under the drum part. Legato would be like adding a deep, solid color to that backdrop. Long notes add to the harmony and fill in the holes, adding a full, thick aspect to the groove.

I'll play some examples using staccato and legato notes. The first example will be a straight eighth-note line, but I'll play every other note staccato. The first time you hear it, the line will be played straight. I'll add staccato notes the second and third times through.

TRACK 54

Play this straight first, then try it with staccato.

TRACK 55

With this one, paint a big, solid backdrop of legato notes.

TRACK 55
(cont'd)

Here I'll mix and match.

TRACK 55
(cont'd)

Dynamics

Dynamics are, essentially, volume. In a song, playing louder during the chorus and softer in the verses is usually standard dynamics protocol. Dynamics are also an overall concept, the big picture. Within that big picture, which we'll call the bass line, how and where you place dynamics on each note will affect the groove. The ability to execute notes dynamically with the plucking or slapping hand is an art within itself. To show you how effective dynamics can be, listen to this next example. First I'll play it at one dynamic level. The second time, I'll add dynamics, by accenting beats two and four. These will be notated with accent marks (>).

TRACK 56

Technically speaking, playing loud is easier than playing soft. Soft volumes are more difficult to accomplish than it may initially seem. Having control and executing notes quietly is critical to a clean, vibrant sound. If you are already playing loud and hard and want to accent a note, you'll have to play even harder. Often times this comes out sounding sloppy and uncontrolled. The next few exercises will concentrate on quiet (Q) and medium (M) dynamics. I'll be plucking these notes.

TRACK 57

TRACK 57
(cont'd)

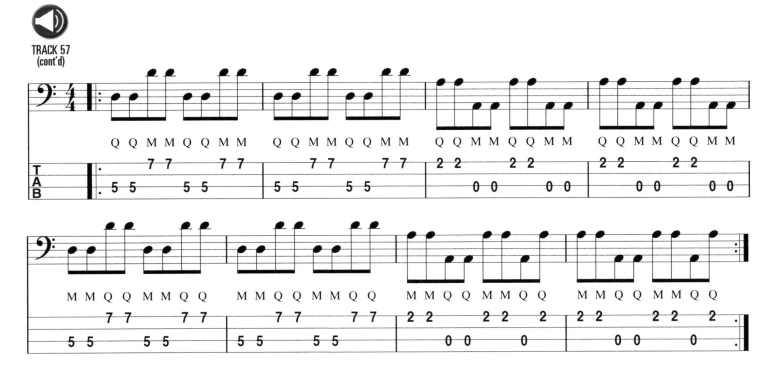

Dynamic Groove

Now that you've worked on the execution of dynamics with your plucking/slapping hand, let's put it to use. In most cases, particularly in jazz and blues, accenting on beats two and four makes the groove happen in a big way. The same goes for most funk songs, especially songs with harmonically active bass lines. A single well-placed accent goes a long way in a groove. If you are playing a bass line and it is not grooving, try placing an accent. You'll develop this concept with experience and experimentation.

Here are two examples with accents on beats two and four.

TRACK 59

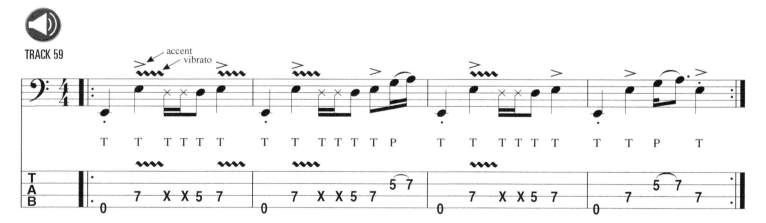

Now try these examples where I've added accents on beats one and three.

TRACK 60

TRACK 60
(cont'd)

The Pocket

Another term used in music related to bass and drums is "the pocket." Remember the musician's definition of groove? Well the pocket is essentially the same thing, but with the added twist that, while playing in the pocket you have some room to shift the timing of the notes just a little bit. Bassists talk about pushing or pulling the groove or pocket. You can push and pull the timing without speeding up or slowing down the song as a whole. There are three ways to play the pocket, you can push, play right on, or pull. This is an art and takes a real great time feel to accomplish; some players do it without even realizing it. The first step is awareness. Let's take a look at the concepts of dragging without slowing down and pushing without speeding up. It's extremely subtle but extremely effective.

Push

Pushing or subtly playing ahead of the beat gives a driving impression to the feel. If a groove is missing that drive or attitude, try pushing the feel to add that extra aggression to a bass line.

Pull

Pulling or playing subtly behind the beat creates a laid back or smooth feel. In R&B it's very common to "lay back" and let the pocket breathe. This is also called a deep pocket.

Right On

Playing straight and dead on, metronome style in the time of the pocket, is usually just what the doctor ordered. It is a great starting place for any groove, and if it's working, don't mess with it.

Many players are unaware of how they play. This can be the difference between bassists who groove really well and bassists who don't. Playing the pocket is about listening and having good "time feel." When playing with drummers, this can work to your advantage or to your demise. Being able to adapt in different situations can make or break any gig. The bass player, as part of the rhythm section, lays the foundation. If a drummer pulls the pocket and you push the pocket, it can leave the rest of the band wondering what's going on or why it doesn't feel good. Playing the pocket with a drummer is about listening and flowing well with how the drummer is playing the pocket; sometimes it can be magical, and sometimes it needs to be discussed if it isn't happening. Certain styles of music require certain types of feels as well. All human players move around in the pocket. The ability to move with the direction and take charge makes all the difference in the world. When working with a drum machine, the groove will be up to you because the drum machine does not fluctuate in time; if you want a more laid back vibe, pull your bass line a little and see how it feels. It's all about listening and awareness!

Let's try a few exercises. First I'll play right on, then I'll pull, and finally push. I'll play to a drum machine so that you can hear how your own bass playing can effect the groove.

57

Confidence

Playing with confidence is everything in funk. If you play timidly, then that is how you will sound. Bass is up front in funk, and the more you play with confidence, the more you will groove. It is better to play the wrong bass line with confidence and attitude than to play the right bass line with fear and timidity. A great way to ground yourself in your playing is to hum or sing your bass line. This will help to internalize what you are playing. Then take what you feel or hear inside and "transcend" this into your bass through your fingertips. Another way is to picture how the funkiest bass player in the world would play the bass line that you are trying, and play it like he would. You will make mistakes, but that is only part of learning. When you do make a mistake, let it go, and keep laying down that line with confidence. Everybody makes mistakes, and as a bassist, the biggest mistake is to not be there as the foundation because you are afraid of making a mistake. Fear is your only enemy.

Triplet or Swing Feel

When grooving, a rhythmic feel called a triplet (swing or shuffle feel) can really enhance a bass line and bring it to life. It can add a bouncy feel to your groove. Triplets subdivide a rhythmic unit (such as a quarter note) into three parts instead of two parts (like an eighth-note triplet instead of the more standard two eighth notes). The figure below will help explain the notational mathematics involved, though it's a concept better understood with the ears than the eyes.

Triplet or shuffle notation would be hard to read so you'll often see straight eighth notes with the word "swing" or written at the beginning of a song. Here is an example of a triplet feel on a straight eighth-note groove. I'll play it straight the first time, then I'll add the triplet feel the second time.

TRACK 63

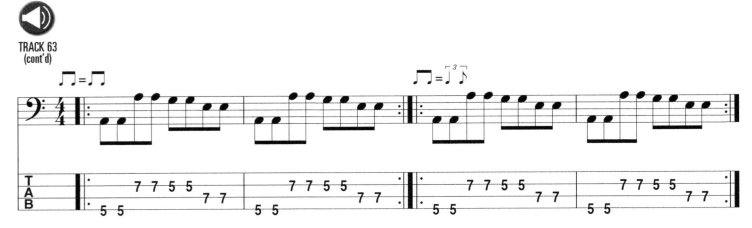

TRACK 63
(cont'd)

58

Let's try a few funk shuffle examples. You'll notice I've been playing this feel in previous examples already. Sometimes when you play it is an instinctual thing, and that is where you will want to be.

TRACK 64

TRACK 64
(cont'd)

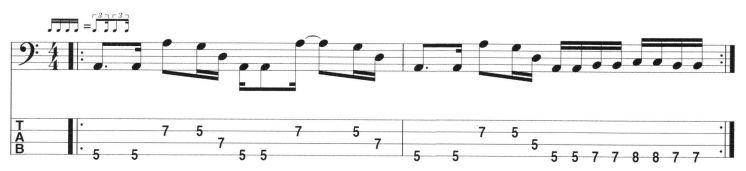

Establishing a Groove

When establishing a groove the first thing to do is listen! Play simply and get the feel. Determine the flow of the pocket. Going through this checklist might help:

- Is it already grooving?
- Would adding accents on certain beats enhance the groove?
- Should you lay back or push? Or keep it where it is?
- Can you add a little swing to the line?
- Are you playing with confidence?

The funny thing is that most players will play more notes when things aren't happening instead of asking themselves these sorts of questions first. Grooving is about feel and vibe, not about the number of notes played or the technique used. The subtle things make all the difference. Build from the bottom up, not from the top down!

Repetition

Groove and foundation in funk are based on repetition. If you choose not to play the same thing over and over to support the feel, then maybe you shouldn't be playing bass. Playing the same line over and over with the same intensity and consistency makes you a strong player. You are laying the foundation; other players can't build on top of that foundation if it keeps moving around.

Fills

When and if you choose to add a fill, make sure it enhances the music and that it's not about throwing in that new slap lick that you just learned. The bottom line is if you're going to fill, make sure it's in time, and don't lose the pocket in the process.

A great way to practice fills and repetition is to play a riff, and every four or eight measures, throw in a fill. Be aware of how well you can stay in time (and in the pocket) as you continue this cycle. For this next exercise, I'll play a one-measure bass line for seven measures, and on the eighth measure, I'll throw in a fill. Do this type of exercise often when practicing; it helps your feel, consistency, and timing.

TRACK 65

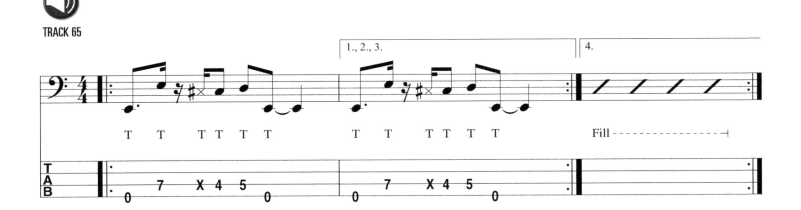

Try playing these songs which all have really strong grooves. This first song has a great feel; the pocket is so deep everyone listening will fall in! This is a Maxwell song entitled "Sumthin' Sumthin'."

TRACK 66

SUMTHIN' SUMTHIN'

Intro

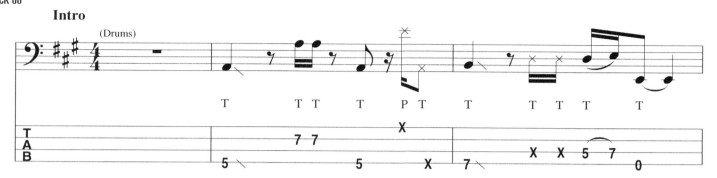

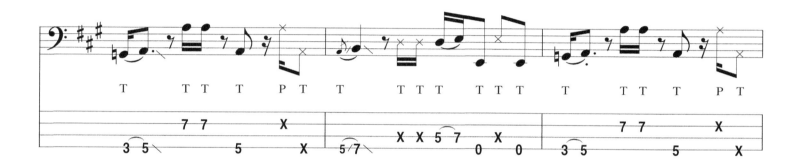

Verse

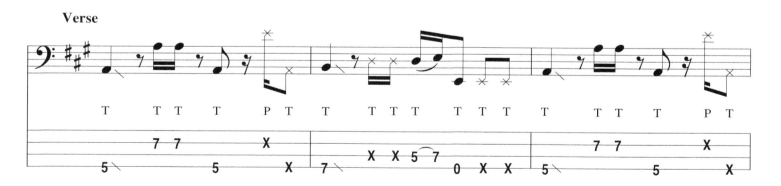

Bass Break

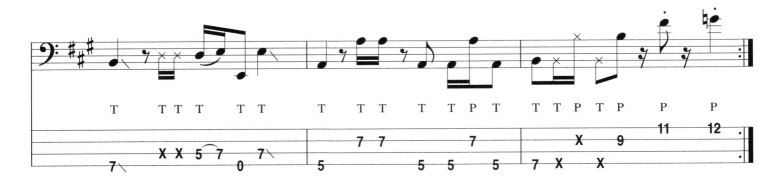

Outro

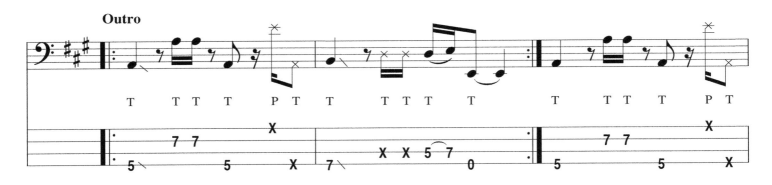

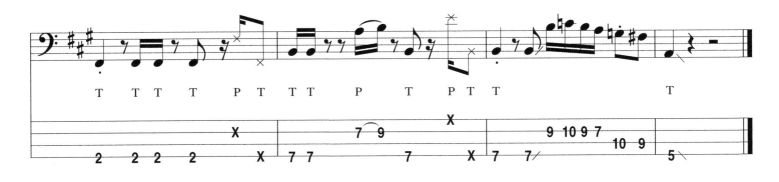

This is a song written and recorded by Chaka Kahn and later covered by Erykah Badu called "Stay." Check out this groove.

STAY

TRACK 67

Play 3 times

Chorus

FINGERSTYLE FUNK

Fingerstyle funk was the start of it all. It began in the mid '60s when bands started giving rhythm and blues a new sound by accenting the drums and bass. Artists like James Brown, Sly and The Family Stone, Kool and The Gang, and Parliament were a few of the pioneers of this musical style. Bassists like Bootsy Collins and James Jamerson set the tone, opening the doors to players such as Rocco Prestia, who added his newer style to funk bass.

Bootsy Collins

James Jamerson

Rocco Prestia

Technique

Since playing funk is more about groove and less about technique, let's explore some ways to enhance your fingerstyle playing. It's an open door because, technically speaking, there is no "right" way to play fingerstyle. However you choose to play with your plucking hand, this section of the book will help you to clean things up, and have more control over dynamics and muting, ultimately helping you to develop better overall execution.

Most players concentrate on the fretting hand and just let the plucking hand follow along. This may work in some cases, but most often the plucking hand's execution is lazy, unclean, and slow. So let's break it down and look at your plucking hand execution. Remember it's all about awareness. If you know what your hands are doing, then you can forget about them and play instinctively without running into roadblocks.

Anchor

Anchoring is about looking at your plucking hand's thumb. When you play on the higher strings, do you anchor your thumb, or does it move around? There is no one correct way; but it's best to commit to a way and stick to it, to be consistent. Choose whether you will anchor your thumb on the pickup, or move your thumb and anchor it on the lower strings. When anchoring your thumb on the pickup, ringing strings and muting might be an issue. If your thumb floats and anchors on the lower strings, it may take more thought and time to pluck, but the open strings can be muted with your thumb as it moves to anchor on them.

Anchor: Pickup w/
Low String Pluck

Anchor: Pickup w/
High String Pluck

Anchor: Floating w/
Low String Pluck

Anchor: Floating w/
High String Pluck

Follow Through

Whether you pluck with two or three fingers, how much do you move your fingers when plucking? One common technique that really helps speed and clarity is follow through. Are your movements minimal or are they exaggerated? The key to a great sound and flawless execution is to have as little movement as possible. You don't want to pluck by pulling the string up or pushing the string down. What you are looking for is a precise flat pluck towards your chest. To work on follow through, try plucking the A string with the first finger and have it follow through to the E string below, allowing the E string to stop your finger. Do the same with your second finger and you'll notice that your fingers only move as far as the spacing between strings. Minimal movement and good control with the plucking hand will help to create a nice, thick, and clean tone.

1. Pluck: 1st Finger

2. Pluck: 2nd Finger

3. Pluck: 1st Finger

Alternating

As stated before, most bassists are unaware of what their plucking fingers are doing. For speed and execution, make sure that you alternate the plucking fingers. If you are using a two-finger technique, make sure that you alternate back and forth between the first and second finger with every pluck.

To push this concept of economy of motion even further, as soon as you pluck with the first finger, place your second finger on the string you just plucked to stop it from ringing. Alternate by doing this back and forth and you'll notice that with every pluck, your second finger is ready to play as soon as you've plucked the previous note. It should sound like this:

TRACK 68

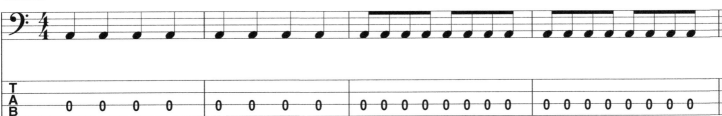

Let's work on some exercises to drive home a solid foundation of finger funk technique. Remember to use as little movement as possible; alternate your plucking fingers and be conscious of your plucking hand's movement. Go back to the prior chapter with this in mind and play those exercises again. It's very important to be conscious of what your plucking fingers are doing.

TRACK 69

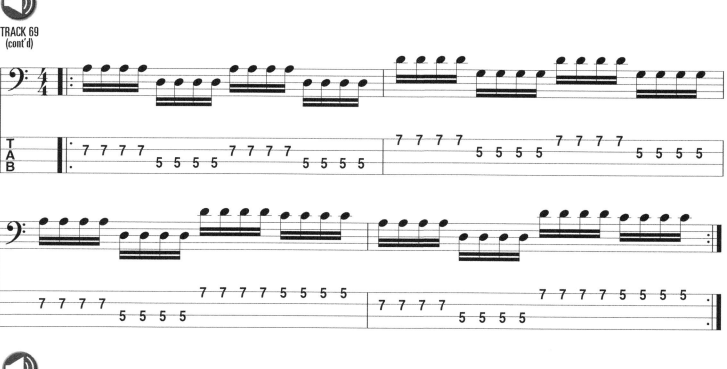

TRACK 70

TRACK 70
(cont'd)

Dead Notes

With fingerstyle, dead notes are a big help in enhancing your funk playing. They move air and add a rhythmic aspect to a line without filling harmonic space. You've already worked on dead note slaps and pops, so let's move into fingerstyle dead notes. The key to making dead notes effective with fingerstyle is to play them with a louder dynamic, since they have no harmonic sound.

TRACK 71

TRACK 71
(cont'd)

TRACK 72

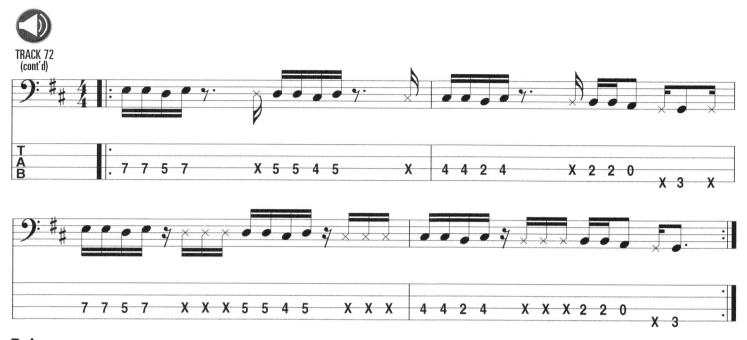

Rake

A rake is another great dead note technique that adds a rhythmic fill without being overbearing. It's a nice drop into the down-beat of a song. All you do is simply mute the strings with your fretting hand, and quickly run a plucking finger across (or "rake") the strings from high to low.

1. Rake: High   2. Rake: Mid   3. Rake: Low

Let's try the rake. Here are a few examples.

TRACK 73

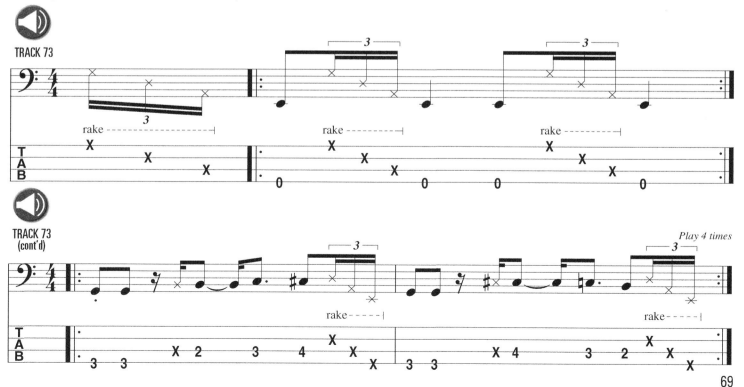

TRACK 73
(cont'd)

Review

Let's go back and review some of the techniques we've learned in the slap and pop style and apply them to a fingerstyle format.

Here is another funk bass classic by The Average White Band called, "Pick Up the Pieces."

PICK UP THE PIECES

TRACK 77

Words and Music by James Hamish Stuart, Alan Gorrie, Roger Ball, Robbie McIntosh, Owen McIntyre and Malcolm Duncan
© 1974 (Renewed 2002) AVERAGE MUSIC (ASCAP)/Administered by BUG MUSIC and JOE'S SONGS, INC. (ASCAP)
All Rights Reserved   Used by Permission

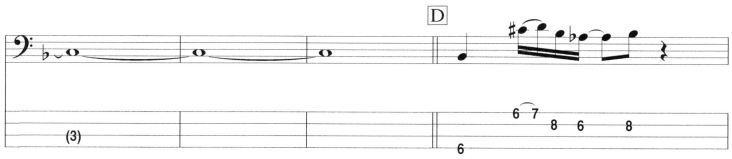

Slap and Fingerstyle

In most funk songs you'll hear a mixture of slap and pop and fingerstyle. Fingerstyle is basically the foundational technique for most bass lines in songs, whereas slap and pop can be a great enhancer to those sections that need a little spice or dynamic increase. Just like anything in music, listen first and start out simple. What kind of bass line do you hear, is it fingerstyle or slap, or a combination of both techniques? Try to follow the needs of the song, not the needs of your ego, then you'll be less apt to throw something in that doesn't belong.

When playing both styles within a song, you may notice a physical change in the positions that you are holding the bass. Most players angle their headstock up slightly when playing fingerstyle, but for slap, they'll drop the headstock to a horizontal level to gain more efficient positioning for thumb slaps and pops.

Let's play some songs that have slap and pop mixed with fingerstyle. This song is by Jamiroquai and is called "Virtual Insanity."

TRACK 78

VIRTUAL INSANITY

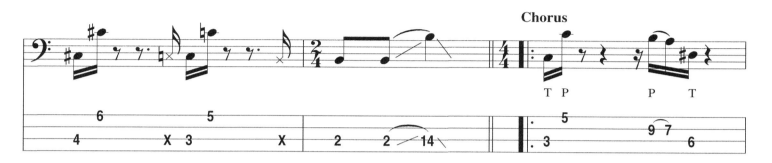

Chorus

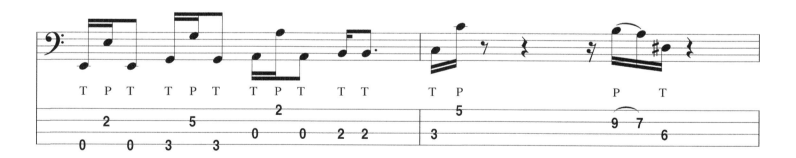

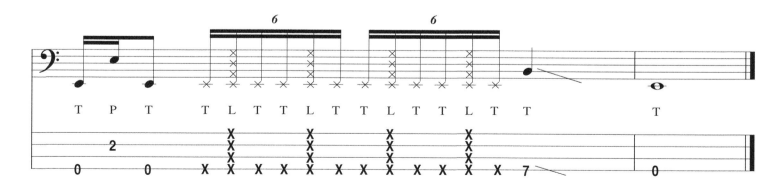

ADVANCED TECHNIQUES

In this chapter let's look at some advanced techniques that can really enhance a groove, but can also ruin one if overused. A big note of caution, use these techniques sparingly… but have some fun pushing your musical envelope.

Over the past thirty years, bass has evolved into an instrument that not only holds down the bottom end, but steps forward to solo as well. Bass masters like Jaco Pastorius, Stanley Clarke, Stuart Hamm, and Victor Wooten, to name a few, have taken the art of bass and pushed it into the forefront with some jaw-dropping musicality and techniques. These techniques can be used in solos, fills, or as a platform for solo bass pieces.

Stanley Clarke

Stuart Hamm

Victor Wooten

Photo by Neil Zlozower

Photo by Neil Zlozower

Photo by Michael Weintrob

Advanced Pops

Finger pops can be used in succession to add a new rhythmic element: a quick, "drum-like" flam sound using two or three fingers.

Double Pop

The double pop is just that, popping the string twice instead of once. Usually this is accomplished by using the first and second fingers of the plucking hand. Start with a thumb slap, then pop with the first finger, followed by the second.

1. Double Pop: Thumb Slap

2. Double Pop: 1st Finger

3. Double Pop: 2nd Finger

Let's try a double pop in a few exercises.

TRACK 79

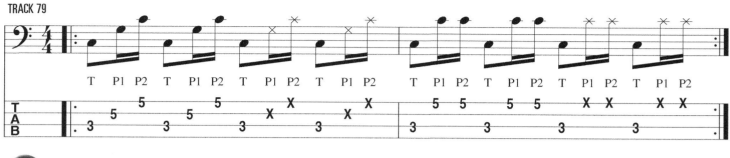

TRACK 79
(cont'd)

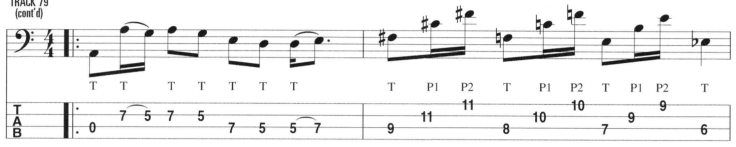

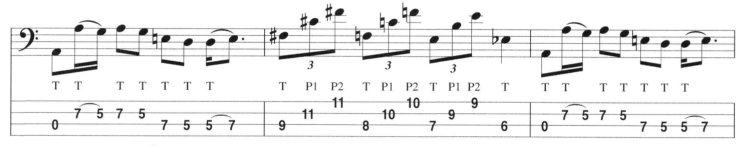

Triple Pop

This is the same as the double pop but with the third finger added into the mix.

Let's try the triple pop in an exercise.

TRACK 80

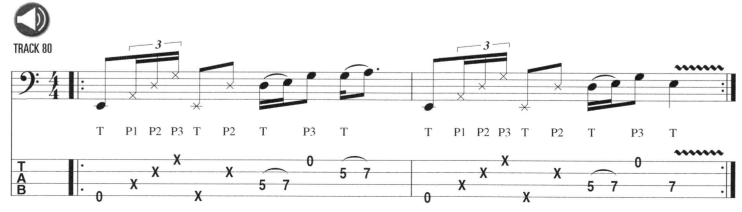

Thumb Slap and Pop

This next technique can be a bit tricky. I want you to try using your thumb like a pick, with a downstroke, then an upstroke, but doing it slap style. First slap down with your thumb, following through with the down slap until your thumb is under the string. Then pull back up with the thumb, adding a subtle thumb pop onto the slap.

1. Thumb Slap and Pop: Setup

2. Thumb Slap and Pop: Slap

3. Thumb Slap and Pop: Follow Through

4. Thumb Slap and Pop: Upstroke Pop

Now let's move into some simple exercises to get the thumb pop down.

TRACK 81

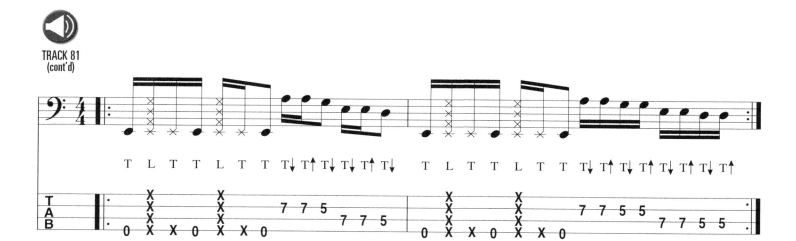

Here's a triplet thumb pop with a finger pop. Practice this one slowly, and as you get comfortable with the movement, it will become easier and more fluid.

TRACK 82

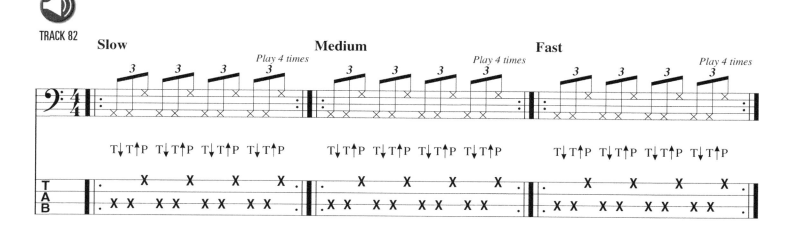

Now I'll add the triplet to a groove.

TRACK 83

Finger Slaps

There are a many, many ways to get percussive sounds out of your bass. As long as it adds to the feel, it's open game. Another percussive method for slapping the strings (other than with the thumb) is the finger slap. This is a great way to add more consecutive slaps than what could be done with the thumb alone. You can perform the same slap action with your slapping hand, but instead using your index, middle, and/or third finger(s) to slap the strings. You can use these finger slaps individually or as slap combinations, depending on the effect you are trying to create.

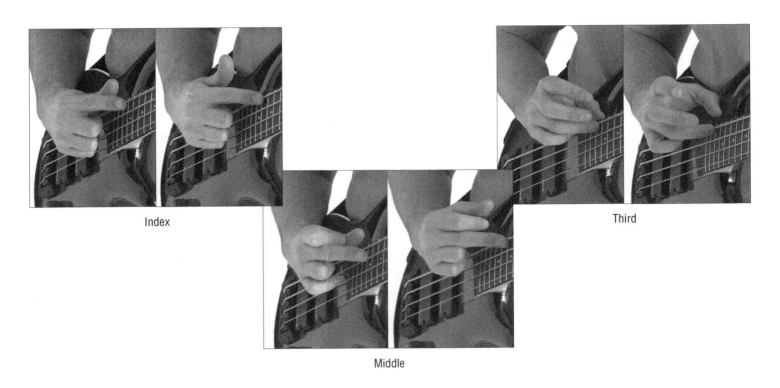

Index

Third

Middle

If you use this technique in multiple finger combinations, try slapping the strings in a successively upward movement (toward your chest): third, middle, then index. Try to achieve a flowing motion.

1. Setup

2. Third

3. Middle

4. Index

So you can hear how this sounds, first I'll play middle and index finger slaps, followed by third, middle, and index finger slaps.

TRACK 84

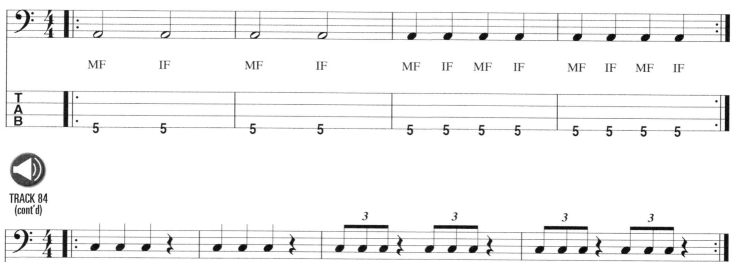

TRACK 84
(cont'd)

Let's try some exercises and throw the thumb in the mix as well.

TRACK 85

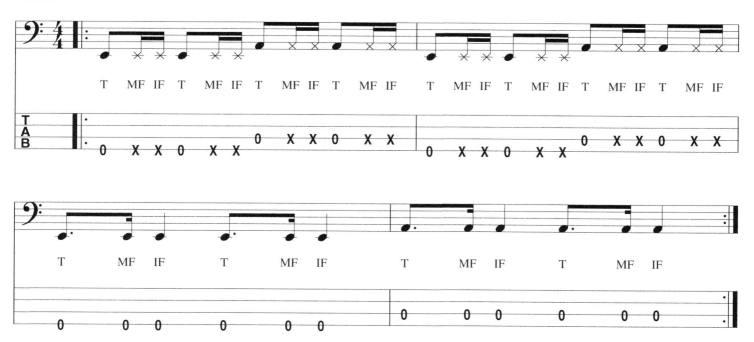

TRACK 85
(cont'd)

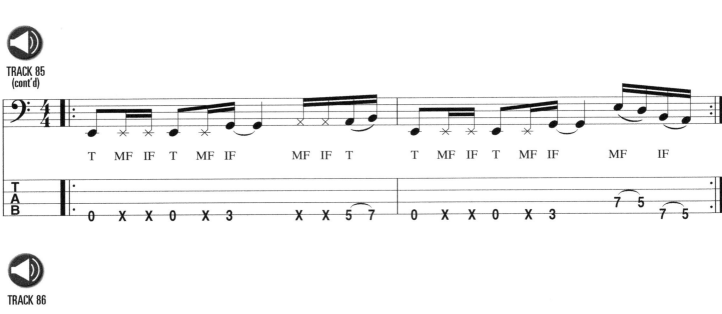

TRACK 86

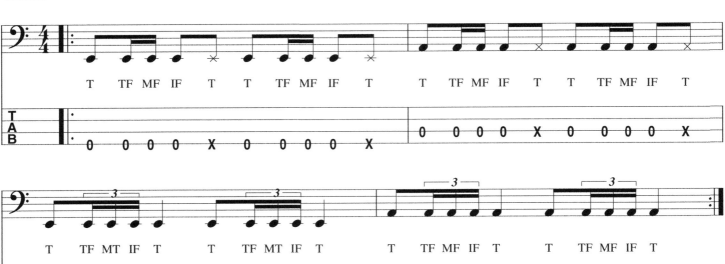

TRACK 86
(cont'd)

Here are a few songs that use these different slap styles. This is an excerpt of a Victor Wooten song called "Sex in a Pan."

This song is palm muted throughout. Palm muting is achieved by resting your plucking hand on your bridge to slightly mute the strings. The thumb and plucking are played dynamically much softer in this excerpt.

SEX IN A PAN

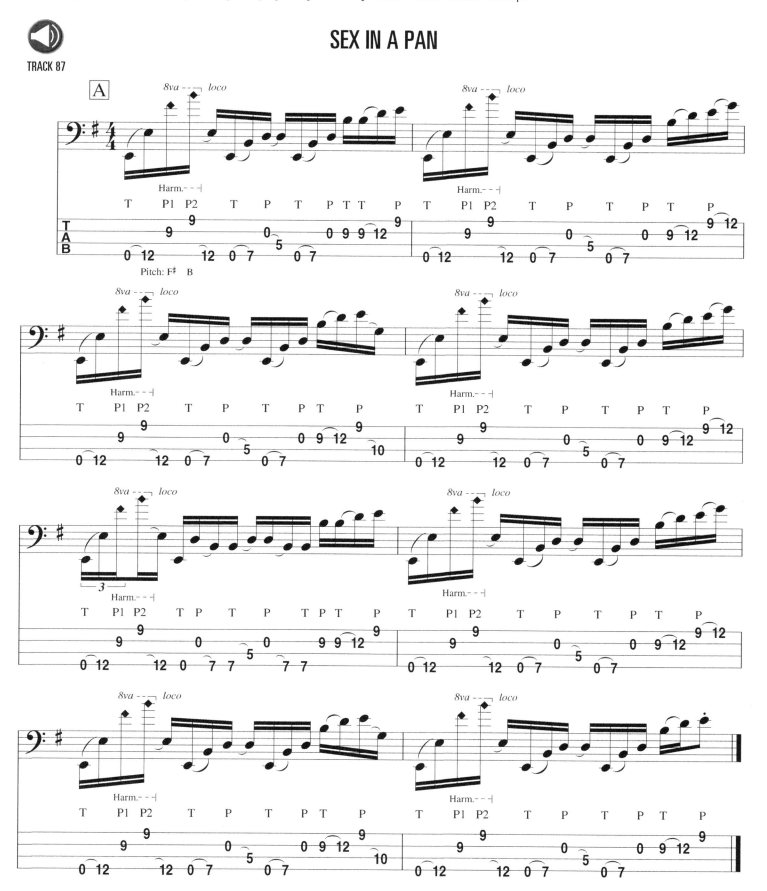

FUNK BASS SOLOING

As a bassist you probably spend most of your time in the pocket, supporting other players while the melody and solos happen. When it comes time for you to solo, it can be a pretty frightening thing. Most of your time is spent working on the groove and holding down the fort. When practicing, this alone can keep you busy for a lifetime. Soloing adds a whole new set of tools to your toolbox. For this you will need to look at technical development, along with melody, chord structure, rhythm, and presence. If you've only got a crescent wrench in your toolbox, there will only be certain things you'll be able to fix, if you follow my analogy. What you'll want is a toolbox full of different tools to use. The fun then comes from trying the new tools out and discovering how they can work in certain situations, as well as learning when and where to use them. Soloing is a huge topic which could take an entire book of its own to cover thoroughly. But due to the nature of this book in covering the funk idiom, we'll only take a look at some of the basics of soloing in the funk style. Let's add a few more tools to the toolbox!

Harmony

Studying music harmony is a necessary skill. The less you know, the more limited you are. Being able to understand keys, scales, chords, and how they relate and work together in a piece of music really makes your playing come together. Along with listening and having a good ear, harmony is a core building block in helping you to become a great player. Throughout this next section, I'll assume you've had some harmony experience and I will only briefly review some basic harmony. If this seems too tough, or if you are new to harmony, I'd suggest that you purchase some Hal Leonard method books that cover harmony in a more detailed fashion so that you can truly understand what I'm only going to review.

Keys

This chart shows the major keys and their corresponding minor keys. If you understand this chart thoroughly you will know what notes to play when someone says, "This song is in the key of ___."

C major/ A minor	No Sharps or Flats	C, D, E, F, G, A, B
G major/ E minor	One Sharp	G, A, B, C, D, E, F#
D major/ B minor	Two Sharps	D, E, F#, G, A, B, C#
A major/ F# minor	Three Sharps	A, B, C#, D, E, F#, G#
E major/ C# minor	Four Sharps	E, F#, G#, A, B, C#, D#
B major/ G# minor	Five Sharps	B, C#, D#, E, F#, G#, A#
F# major/ D# minor	Six Sharps	F#, G#, A#, B, C#, D#, E#
C# major/ A# minor	Seven Sharps	C#, D#, E#, F#, G#, A#, B#
F major/ D minor	One Flat	F, G, A, B♭, C, D, E
B♭ major/ G minor	Two Flats	B♭, C, D, E♭, F, G, A
E♭ major/ C minor	Three Flats	E♭, F, G, A♭, B♭, C, D
A♭ major/ F minor	Four Flats	A♭, B♭, C, D♭, E♭, F, G
D♭ major/ B♭ minor	Five Flats	D♭, E♭, F, G♭, A♭, B♭, C
G♭ major/ E♭ minor	Six Flats	G♭, A♭, B♭, C♭, D♭, E♭, F
C♭ major/ A♭ minor	Seven Flats	C♭, D♭, E♭, F♭, G♭, A♭, B♭

Scales

The tables below show six scales: Major, Minor, Dominant, Major Pentatonic, Minor Pentatonic, and the Blues scale. All of these scales are movable, which means you can play the finger pattern anywhere on the neck, playing the scale in the key of your starting note!

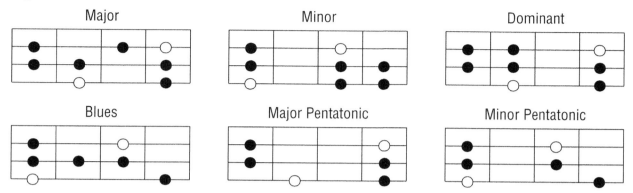

Melody

As a bassist you might feel lacking in the melody department, as you usually concern yourself with rhythm and groove. When beginning to solo, it is great for you to start hearing music in a melodic sense, because what you are trying to do is tell a story with melody. In this next section, let's learn the melodies of some songs and try to play them. A great way to start practicing is to play the melodies you've heard or that you can sing in your head or heart. If you can transfer what you hear in your head to your bass, your playing will sound more natural. The more you play melodically, the more it becomes an integral part of your musical voice. Let's take a look at a few simple examples.

Hopefully you already know these next melodies. Now try transferring them to the bass.

Words by John Newton
From A Collection of Sacred Ballads
Traditional American Melody
From Carrell and Clayton's Virginia Harmony
Arranged by Edwin O. Excell
Copyright © 2004 by HAL LEONARD CORPORATION
International Copyright Secured   All Rights Reserved

How about this one?

TRACK 88
(cont'd)

Now let's take a look at a Marcus Miller solo. Marcus is a great example of a very melodic soloist. He's a master at mixing in the rhythmic aspect of bass with a melody line.

FUNNY

Phrasing

A great way to improve your soloing is by working on your phrasing. Phrasing can be like practicing little solos or fills over a groove while simultaneously working on your timing and execution. Start by breaking down an idea into a riff or groove, then add fills every few measures, and finish with a return to the groove. This really helps develop melodic ideas. You may want to try adding those little slap licks you've thought about and see how they work out.

Here I'll play three measures of a groove, then on the fourth measure, I'll add a fill. After each cycle, I'll return to the groove. This is a great way to practice improvisation.

TRACK 90

Now I'll make the fill time a little longer.

TRACK 91

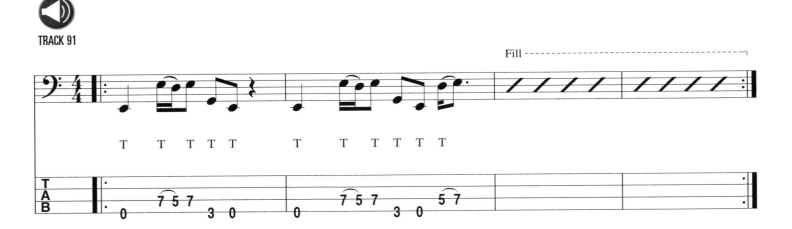

Set up a metronome or drum machine and work on your phrasing.

Motif

Motifs are little melodic or rhythmic ideas that you can build on to create a full-blown solo. The motif is an inherent part of the solo. A place to call home and go back to, it also gives the audience a musical idea to connect with. A motif can be either rhythmic, melodic, or, particularly in a bass solo, a mix of the two.

Here is a commonly used rhythmic motif to build on in a solo.

TRACK 92

This one is a melodic motif that I'll embellish. Listen to how it develops.

TRACK 93

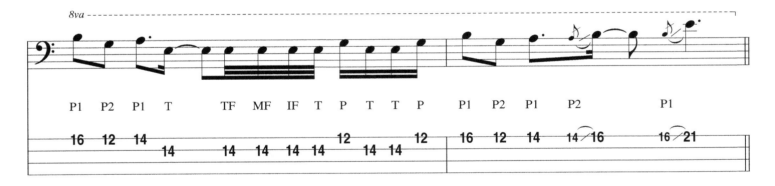

If you are having a hard time with the concept of motifs, try thinking less and listening more. The key is to open up your ears. Play a motif, then stop and try singing what your heart knows should come next. After you've sung it, try playing what you've sung. Try this exercise and you might find that all those years of playing and listening to music have given you pretty clear ideas of what you want to hear next. In this next exercise you'll hear a simple melody, and after I've played it, try singing what you know should come next, and finish by playing what you've just sung.

TRACK 94

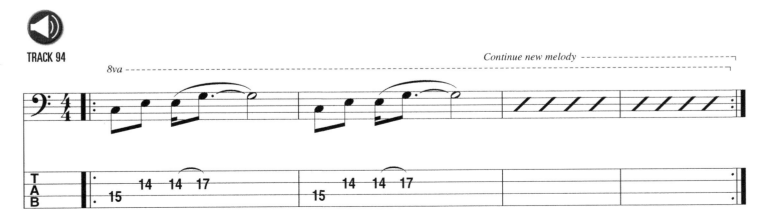

This time I'll mix up a melodic and rhythmic motif and build on that.

TRACK 95

Building a Solo

Building a solo is like using all the ideas, melodies, phrasings, motifs, and techniques to build a grand house from the foundation up. Tell a story, build a house, paint a picture, whatever you'd like to call it; when you build or create something, it usually starts out small and simple, building on that to take you someplace in the middle, and closing with a big or dramatic ending. Use all of your tools in building that solo, from dynamics to technique, melody to harmony. My best advice is to start out simple and build from there.

Here is a solo from the song "Love and Happiness." Listen to how he starts, where he takes it, and how he ends.

TRACK 96

LOVE AND HAPPINESS

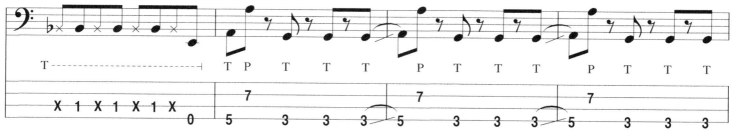

Bass Solo

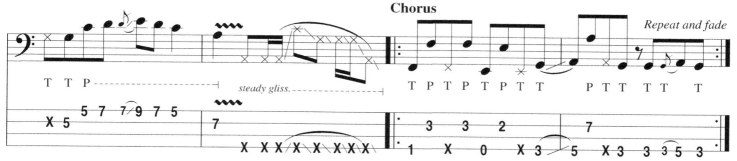

Check out this bass solo in the final example. Once you've listened to the track, pan the bass over so it's silent and then play along and try out your own solo.

TRACK 97

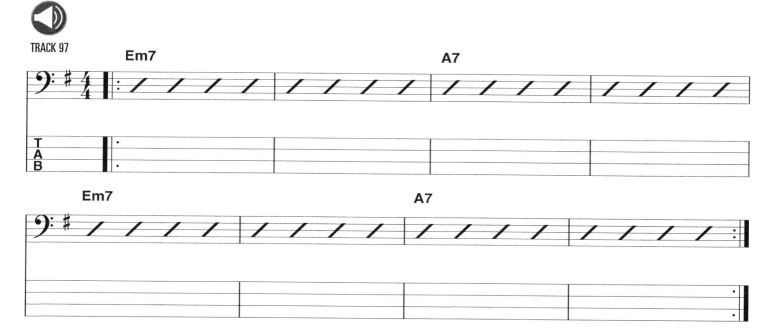

Chops

Chops is a word used by musicians to describe technically advanced playing. Having chops or great technical skill is a blessing, but it can be misused in place of musical wherewithal. A place to strive for is being musical with everything you do, and having the chops to enhance your musical statement. Music is art. Remember that whatever you play is your art and no one else's. Musicians have opinions about what other musicians do. Is one player's music really "bad," or is it more a matter of personal taste? If you keep in mind why you play what you play, and for whom you play, you will continue to advance on your musical path and develop your chops.

Grooving a Solo

When in doubt, groove! If you are having a hard time with soloing, then just groove through your time in the spotlight. Some of the best solos are simple and just groovy. Your role as a funk bassist is to play in the pocket, and if you get a chance to solo, you may choose to say what you want to say musically by continuing to groove hard!

FINAL WORDS

Basses

This book was written with funk bass playing in mind. That being said, the book is more about the fretted electric bass, rather than the fretless electric bass or acoustic upright. In choosing a bass to best recreate that funk sound, you may want to consider what instruments your favorite bassists or artists use to get their tone. There are so many basses on the market today that it can be stupefying. There's a lot of different brands with a lot of different options, including active or passive electronics, not to mention 4, 5, 6, or even 7 strings! The playability of these instruments is a matter of personal taste and tone, so find a bass that is comfortable for you and sounds good. Your favorite player's instrument might not even fit with what you are looking for.

A few classic funk basses to check out are the Fender Jazz bass and the Musicman Stingray bass. These days, with so many basses on the market, the choices are

Fender Jazz   Musicman Stingray   Spector

harder to make. A few great current bass brands are Stuart Spector Design, Modulus, Warrior, Ibanez, and Lakeland. These are only a place to start, there are many, many more depending on your personal preferences.

Amplifiers and Speaker Cabinets

Just like basses, there are a massive amount of bass amplifiers on the market. Again, consider what the players or artists whom you admire use for their tone and go from there. You can buy a combo amp, which has an amp and speaker all in one, or you can buy amplifiers and cabinets separately. Separate units are usually more versatile if you want higher wattage or a combination of tones. Amplifiers also come with a variety of options. Among the possibilities are tube, solid state, a combination of tube and solid state, different types of equalizations (parametric or graphic), various built-in effects, and different wattage or power.

Tube amplifiers give you a warmer tone overall, but they do tend to weigh a bit more. The tubes also need to be replaced every few years. But it may be worth dealing with these issues to get the warm tone that tube amps produce. Solid-state amplifiers have a crisper, brighter tone and can be packed into a smaller, more lightweight box. Combination amps, with tubes and solid-state, usually have a tube pre-amp section and a solid-state power section, which gives you the best of both worlds, the warmth of the tubes and the brightness of solid state. The combination amps can also make for a lighter, more compact setup. Power handling or wattage depends on the way you play and how loud you need to be onstage and at rehearsals. For a small setting, 100 to 300 watts is adequate. For bigger or louder needs, 350 to 1,200 watt amps will give you more than enough power.

Speaker cabinets have come a long way in the past few years. They are much more compact, versatile, and able to handle higher wattage than ever before. Speaker cabinets come in a variety of speaker combinations, anything from 1x12, to 2x10, 2x12, 1x15, 1x18, 4x10, even 8x8 inch speakers! Most cabinets now have a horn or tweeter as well to help produce the crisp highs.

When deciding on what you need, try out several brands, consider your budget, and open your ears; decide what sounds good to you. Several brands specializing in bass amplification are Eden, SWR, Gallien-Krueger, Hartke, Aguilar, Ampeg, and Trace Elliot. Don't forget Peavey and Fender, who make not only bass cabinets, but PA gear and musical instruments as well.

SWR

Hartke

Euphonic Audio

Thank you for purchasing Hal Leonard's Funk Bass Method. I hope this book gave you an in-depth look at the funk bass approach, especially slap and pop style, grooving, and soloing.

Remember that the number one role of the bassist is to groove and stay in the pocket. When it comes time to step forward and fill or solo, if you can't do it in time, don't do it at all.

Learning bass or music of any kind is not an overnight thing. Wisdom and learning comes from experience and practice, and most of all, time. Enjoy the journey and forgive yourself for the mistakes you will make, because in the end, they will make you a stronger, better player. Remember to balance your playing; if you have a lot of chops and technique comes easily to you, remember to then work on your ears and harmony. It's all about balance. Most of all have fun, and keep it exciting!

HAL LEONARD
BASS METHOD

METHOD BOOKS

by Ed Friedland

BOOK 1

Book 1 teaches: tuning; playing position; musical symbols; notes within the first five frets; common bass lines, patterns and rhythms; rhythms through eighth notes; playing tips and techniques; more than 100 great songs, riffs and examples; and more! The audio includes 44 full-band tracks for demonstration or play-along.
00695067 Book Only..............................$7.99
00695068 Book/Online Audio................$12.99

BOOK 2

Book 2 continues where Book 1 left off and teaches: the box shape; moveable boxes; notes in fifth position; major and minor scales; the classic blues line; the shuffle rhythm; tablature; and more!
00695069 Book Only..............................$7.99
00695070 Book/Online Audio................$12.99

BOOK 3

With the third book, progressing students will learn more great songs, riffs and examples; sixteenth notes; playing off chord symbols; slap and pop techniques; hammer-ons and pull-offs; playing different styles and grooves; and more.
00695071 Book Only..............................$7.99
00695072 Book/Online Audio................$12.99

COMPOSITE

This money-saving edition contains Books 1, 2 and 3.
00695073 Book Only..............................$17.99
00695074 Book/Online Audio................$24.99

DVD

Play your favorite songs in no time with this DVD! Covers: tuning, notes in first through third position, rhythms through eighth notes, fingerstyle and pick playing, 4/4 and 3/4 time, and more! Includes 6 full songs and on-screen music notation. 68 minutes.
00695849 DVD $19.95

BASS FOR KIDS

by Chad Johnson

Bass for Kids is a fun, easy course that teaches children to play bass guitar faster than ever before. Popular songs such as "Crazy Train," "Every Breath You Take," "A Hard Day's Night" and "Wild Thing" keep kids motivated, and the clean, simple page layouts ensure their attention remains focused on one concept at a time.
00696449 Book/Online Audio $12.99

REFERENCE BOOKS

BASS SCALE FINDER

by Chad Johnson

Learn to use the entire fretboard with the *Bass Scale Finder*. This book contains over 1,300 scale diagrams for the most important 17 scale types.
00695781 6" x 9" Edition.......................$7.99
00695778 9" x 12" Edition.....................$7.99

BASS ARPEGGIO FINDER

by Chad Johnson

This extensive reference guide lays out over 1,300 arpeggio shapes. 28 different qualities are covered for each key, and each quality is presented in four different shapes.
00695817 6" x 9" Edition.......................$7.99
00695816 9" x 12" Edition.....................$7.99

MUSIC THEORY FOR BASSISTS

by Sean Malone

Acclaimed bassist and composer Sean Malone will explain the written language of music, using easy-to-understand terms and concepts, diagrams, and much more. The audio provides 96 tracks of examples, demonstrations, and play-alongs.
00695756 Book/Online Audio $17.99

STYLE BOOKS

BASS LICKS

by Ed Friedland

This comprehensive supplement to any bass method will help students learn over 200 great bass licks, lines and grooves in many rhythmic styles. *Bass Licks* illustrates how simple melodic patterns can become the springboard for group improvisation or the foundation of a song.
00696035 Book/Online Audio $14.99

BASS LINES

by Matt Scharfglass

500 expertly written bass lines, riffs and fills in a wide variety of musical genres are included in this comprehensive collection to help players expand their bass vocabulary. The examples cover many tempos, keys and feels, and include easy bass lines for beginners on up to advanced riffs for more experienced bassists.
00148194 Book/Online Audio $19.99

BLUES BASS

by Ed Friedland

Learn to play studying the songs of B.B. King, Stevie Ray Vaughan, Muddy Waters, Albert King, the Allman Brothers, T-Bone Walker, and many more. Learn riffs from blues classics including: Born Under a Bad Sign • Hideaway • Hoochie Coochie Man • Killing Floor • Pride and Joy • Sweet Home Chicago • The Thrill Is Gone • and more.
00695870 Book/Online Audio $14.99

COUNTRY BASS

by Glenn Letsch

21 songs, including: Act Naturally • Boot Scootin' Boogie • Crazy • Honky Tonk Man • Love You Out Loud • Luckenbach, Texas (Back to the Basics of Love) • No One Else on Earth • Ring of Fire • Southern Nights • Streets of Bakersfield • Whose Bed Have Your Boots Been Under? • and more.
00695928 Book/Online Audio $17.99

FRETLESS BASS

by Chris Kringel

18 songs, including: Bad Love • Continuum • Even Flow • Everytime You Go Away • Hocus Pocus • I Could Die for You • Jelly Roll • King of Pain • Kiss of Life • Lady in Red • Tears in Heaven • Very Early • What I Am • White Room • more.
00695850..$19.99

FUNK BASS

by Chris Kringel

This is your complete guide to learning the basics of grooving and soloing funk bass. Songs include: Can't Stop • I'll Take You There • Let's Groove • Stay • What Is Hip • and more.
00695792 Book/Online Audio..............$22.99

R&B BASS

by Glenn Letsch

This book/audio pack uses actual classic R&B, Motown, soul and funk songs to teach you how to groove in the style of James Jamerson, Bootsy Collins, Bob Babbitt, and many others. The 19 songs include: For Once in My Life • Knock on Wood • Mustang Sally • Respect • Soul Man • Stand by Me • and more.
00695823 Book/Online Audio $17.99

ROCK BASS

by Sean Malone

This book/audio pack uses songs from a myriad of rock genres to teach the key elements of rock bass. Includes: Another One Bites the Dust • Beast of Burden • Money • Roxanne • Smells like Teen Spirit • and more.
00695801 Book/Online Audio..............$21.99

SUPPLEMENTARY SONGBOOKS

These great songbooks correlate with Books 1-3 of the *Hal Leonard Bass Method*, giving students great songs to play while they're still learning! The audio tracks include great accompaniment and demo tracks.

EASY POP BASS LINES

20 great songs that students in Book 1 can master. Includes: Come as You Are • Crossfire • Great Balls of Fire • Imagine • Surfin' U.S.A. • Takin' Care of Business • Wild Thing • and more.
00695810 Book Only..............................$9.99
00695809 Book/Online Audio..............$15.99

MORE EASY POP BASS LINES

20 great songs for Level 2 students. Includes: Bad, Bad Leroy Brown • Crazy Train • I Heard It Through the Grapevine • My Generation • Pride and Joy • Ramblin' Man • Summer of '69 • and more.
00695819 Book Only..............................$12.99
00695818 Book/Online Audio..............$16.99

EVEN MORE EASY POP BASS LINES

20 great songs for Level 3 students, including: ABC • Another One Bites the Dust • Brick House • Come Together • Higher Ground • Iron Man • The Joker • Sweet Emotion • Under Pressure • more.
00695821 Book.....................................$9.99
00695820 Book/Online Audio..............$16.99